COVOCATIONAL CHURCH PLANTING

ALIGNING YOUR MARKETPLACE CALLING & THE MISSION OF GOD

BY BRAD BRISCO

© 2021 by Brad Brisco

ISBN: 978-1-7362821-1-3

All rights reserved. No part of this publication may be reproduced, distributed, or transmitted in any form or by any means, including photocopying, recording, or other electronic or mechanical methods, without the prior written permission of the publisher, except in the case of brief quotations in critical reviews and certain other noncommercial uses permitted by copyright law.

Cover design by Katie Shull.

Published by:
Missional Press, a subsidiary of 610Media.
Nashville, TN
missionalpressbooks.com

Printed in the United States of America.

COVOCATIONAL CHURCH PLANTING

ALIGNING YOUR MARKETPLACE CALLING & THE MISSION OF GOD

BY BRAD BRISCO

FOREWORD BY HUGH HALTER

MISSIONAL PRESS
-NASHVILLE, TN-

CONTENTS

Foreword..1
Introduction...5

Section One: ReThink
Chapter 1: ReThink Bivocational Church Planting.......................15
Chapter 2: ReThink Church and Mission.....................................23

Section Two: Kingdom Thinking (Christology)
Chapter 3: Recalibrating Back to Jesus..37
Chapter 4: The Gospel of the Kingdom......................................45
Chapter 5: The Kingdom Agenda..53
Chapter 6: Jesus Spirituality..61

Section Three: Missional Engagement (Missiology)
Chapter 7: Place, Prayer and the Person of Peace......................72
Chapter 8: The Spirit in Mission..85
Chapter 9: Engaging First Places...93
Chapter 10: Engaging Second Places..103
Chapter 11: Engaging Third Places..111
Chapter 12: The Power of Biblical Hospitality...........................119
Chapter 13: Missional Discipleship..129
Chapter 14: Incarnational Evangelism.......................................137

Section Four: Biblical Community (Ecclesiology)
Chapter 15: Missionary Flow..150
Chapter 16: Starting Missional Communities................................163
Chapter 17: APEST: Activating All the People of God...................171
Chapter 18: Movement and Multiplication....................................185
Chapter 19: Creating New Scorecards..193

Section Five: Sustainable Life
Chapter 20: Covo Aptitudes...202
Chapter 21: Importance of Margin...215
Chapter 22: Identifying Missional Leaders...................................221

Suggested Reading..230
About the Author...232
Acknowledgements..232
Endnotes..233

FOREWORD

One of the strangest, most counterintuitive stories Jesus ever taught is recorded in Luke 16:8-13. We call it the parable of the shrewd manager. In essence, Jesus commends a slimy, money-grubbing ex-employee for shrewdly—and dishonestly—leveraging old ac- counts for his own gain after the boss fires him. At the end of the parable Jesus says,

> The master commended the dishonest manager because he had acted shrewdly. For the people of this world are more shrewd in dealing with their own kind than are the people of the light. I tell you, use worldly wealth to gain friends for yourselves, so that when it is gone, you will be welcomed into eternal dwellings.
>
> Whoever can be trusted with very little can also be trusted with much, and whoever is dishonest with very little will also be dishonest with much. So if you have not been trustworthy in handling worldly wealth, who will trust you with true riches? And if you have not been trustworthy with someone else's property, who will give you property of your own?

COVOCATIONAL CHURCH PLANTING

> No one can serve two masters. Either you will hate the one and love the other, or you will be devoted to the one and despise the other. You cannot serve both God and money.

Wow. Jesus is rebuking his followers for not being more shrewd, creative or innovative in using money to gain respect and friend- ship with those outside the faith.

Could it be that He might say something similar to us today?

Most good innovations come out of a time of discontent. Until there is a high level of dissatisfaction with the status quo, there isn't a strong reason to try something new or consider an alternative paradigm. So it is with money and mission. For less than 100 years many church leaders have been enjoying a blessing that today, at least at times, may feel like more a curse. We've been able to get paid to do the work of mission.

Prior to this century, the gospel expanded through neighborhoods and networks where most people worked normal jobs, either in the field or in the marketplace. At the same time, they took leadership over growing movements of disciples and churches, mostly small ones.

Today a new breed of leader, and subsequently a new form of church, is emerging that may be the last hope for the future of the church in the North America. I don't say this lightly. Having spent the past 25 years working with countless denominations, traveling more than 2 million air miles and witnessing courageous leaders of brand-new wineskins, I can tell you that money and mission no longer have to have the same relationship they once did.

A tidal wave of young leaders are now choosing to leverage all facets of their life into one focused mission of God. They reject the idea that bivocational funding means you are lousy at both church leadership and a marketplace vocation. They instead believe they can, and in most missionary contexts must, have more than one vocation to both sustain their livelihood and model a form of church that activates all the people of God.

This is why I'm so thankful Brad has taken a term I have often used called "Bivo" and appropriately innovated the concept under the name "Covo."

In Covocational Church Planting, Brad does a masterful job helping us rethink vocation and how it should align with God's mission. But he also provides a beautiful array of options for every man and woman to think and act like a missionary regardless of the calling God has given them.

I hope this resource will be at the front of the line for those who wish to make the kingdom tangible through their marketplace calling, business ventures and the consolidated ethic of work.

– Hugh Halter

Author of *BiVO*, *Flesh*, *The Tangible Kingdom*, and owner of The Post Common, a business venture and church plant in Alton, Ill.

COVOCATIONAL CHURCH PLANTING

INTRODUCTION

If you want to build a ship, don't summon people to buy wood, prepare tools, distribute jobs, and organize the work, rather teach people the yearning for the wide, boundless ocean.

– Antoine de Saint-Exupéry

The organization of this church planting resource is very deliberate. The book is structured in five sections. The first section is simply titled *ReThink*. In the first two chapters, we *rethink* not only the concept of bivocational church planting but we also consider a couple of key theological foundations that should shape the way we think about church planting.

As a result of four decades of church growth thinking, many Christians have developed deeply held assumptions about church and mission that may need to be unlearned and relearned. Without such *realignment*, we run the risk of simply attaching new language to what the church is already doing and ignoring the significant changes, or paradigm shifts, that are necessary. A genuine discipleship focused, bivocational church planting movement is not about tweaking the way we *do* church. Instead, it involves a thorough recalibration of the way we understand God's mission in the world and how the church is created to participate in it.

COVOCATIONAL CHURCH PLANTING

The hearts and minds of the people in local congregations must be captured by a revolutionary way of thinking about and living out the Christian life. This simply will not happen if they don't begin the journey with thoughtful theological reflection. Before we ask *what* we should do, we must first ask *why*. Why does the religious landscape in North America seem to be changing so quickly? Why don't the strategies and models for church growth "work" like they used to? More importantly, why do we need to reconsider the nature and essence of the church? Why does the church in North America need to rethink mission? Why do we need to change the way we live our lives, individually and collectively as the body of Jesus? Addressing questions like these should prompt us to think both theologically and missiologically. As a result, we will begin to think and behave like a missionary. But today the mission field is not in a faraway land; it is in our own backyard.

Starting with theological reflection is the best way to fully understand the practices in which we should be engaging. In other words, this must be a theological process and not simply a pragmatic one. Without serious reflection on the missionary nature of the church, we will not completely grasp the fact that we are all missionaries sent into a local context. Without thinking well on the in- carnation of Jesus, we will not totally comprehend the crucial posture of humility and sacrifice. And without seriously considering the doctrine of the *missio Dei*, we will not recognize the importance of discovery and discernment throughout our missionary engagement. However, in the first section of this book we will only have the space to deal with a couple of these theological foundations. For a more thorough discussion see the e-book titled *ReThink: 9 Key Paradigm Shifts for Activating the Church*.

The second, third and fourth sections of the book are titled Kingdom Thinking, Missional Engagement and Biblical Community. Each of these sections are in a very purposeful order. Our Christology (*Kingdom Thinking*) should determine our missiology (*Missional Engagement*), which in turn should determine our ecclesiology (*Biblical Community*). When we get these three concepts in the wrong order, we often allow our idea of church to

COVOCATIONAL CHURCH PLANTING

govern our sense of purpose and mission. Churches that have this basic formulation wrong often spend too much time discussing (or arguing) about the forms of worship, church structure and types of programs and fail to recognize that our ecclesiology flows more naturally out of a deep sense of mission. Jesus determines our purpose and mission in the world (discipleship), and as we follow Him into that mission we should discover different expressions of being the church.

The Venn diagram below illustrates how these three concepts work together. In addition, it emphasizes the idea that when the church lives out the disciple-making implications of each of the three circles, the natural fruit, represented by the "sweet spot" of the diagram, will be disciple making.

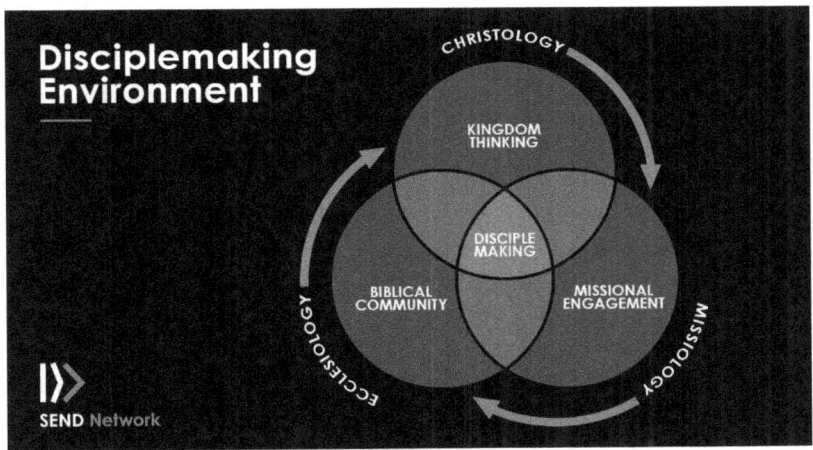

While the more practical aspects of discipleship will be discussed in chapter 13, here I want to help you *rethink* the prominence of disciple making within each of the three circles. The point is that disciple making should be woven into the fabric of every- thing we are and do as the church. It must become the pervasive ethos felt at every level of the organization. And because this Venn diagram illustrates the organization of this book, let's begin by discussing how disciple making must be embedded into each of the three circles.

DISCIPLE MAKING AND KINGDOM THINKING (CHRISTOLOGY)

Disciple making is first and foremost about the centrality of Jesus. Essentially, it involves the lifelong task of becoming more and more like Jesus by embodying His message as well as His practices. Not only was Jesus the perfect model of a disciple maker—He formally invited 12 people to be His disciples (Mark 3:13–19)—but His *ways* are the curriculum for our disciple making. Discipleship is basically a Jesus-saturated affair, through which He lives His life in and through His people (union with Christ), and we become more like Him (imitation of Christ).

The word *apprenticeship* best describes the disciple-making process. If you have never been involved in a trade, the apprenticeship process may not be familiar. Yet the image of being an apprentice communicates many of the key ideas of disciple making. An ap- prentice is a person who is learning by practical experience a trade, art or calling. This is accomplished under the guidance of a skilled worker. The apprentice learns from observing and being in the presence of the one who has experience and wisdom in a particular trade. So, a disciple maker is a person who is apprenticing others into *Kingdom Thinking*, or the likeness of Jesus.

> *He is the one we proclaim, admonishing and teaching everyone with all wisdom, so that we may present everyone fully mature in Christ.*
>
> *–Colossians 1:28*

DISCIPLE MAKING AND MISSIONAL ENGAGEMENT (MISSIOLOGY)

Too often, the missing component in the disciple-making environment is the lack of connecting discipleship and missional engagement. For too long, the church has associated discipleship with the transfer of information, often within the four walls of the church. Further, discipleship has been limited to issues relating to our own personal morality and ethics. In doing this, we have neglected the biblical mandate to *go* and "make disciples." In other words, we have narrowed the gospel message to be just about us.

Now we don't want to neglect issues of personal morality; certainly, discipleship involves striving for holiness and maturity in our own personal lives, but that is only half the picture. The other half is our God-given responsibility to the world around us. How can we be discipled into the *ways* of Jesus without participating in the *mission* of Jesus? He gave instructions to the disciples and then taught them once they had attempted His directives. Jesus was *apprenticing* the disciples in the midst of a constant rhythm of missional action-reflection. The church must do the same. Our disciple-making process cannot be void of missional engagement.

As every member is activated to engage in God's mission, we must create opportunities for them to reflect on their missional involvement. Sometimes this may simply mean we need individual "down time" to reflect upon our activities. We may need to ask God to affirm our involvement or to ask for clarity of direction. But it will also mean carving out time to reflect with others among our faith community. We need to hear what others are seeing and sensing concerning God's activities and to hear the stories of how others are engaging God's mission.

However, not only do we need to reflect on what God is doing "out there" in our missional context, but we need to reflect on what God is doing "in here"—inside of us. We need to ask, how is God shaping and forming our hearts as we engage in His mission? This is a crucial component of discipleship. As we engage in God's mission, the Spirit can transform our hearts. But this transformation also occurs as we each share (apprentice) with each other what God is doing inside of us in the midst of our missional engagement. What is God revealing to me? How is He calling me into His mission in new ways? What am I learning about myself?

DISCIPLE MAKING AND BIBLICAL COMMUNITY (ECCLESIOLOGY)

Missional engagement is best done as a communal activity. As mentioned in the previous paragraph, the rhythm of action-reflection happens best in community. We can't be apprenticed in isolation. Again, our relationship with Jesus is central to everything. Jesus is the teacher, the curriculum and the classroom. However, as social, relational beings, we are created to live the Jesus life in community with other believers.

The crucial interplay of these three aspects of the disciple-making environment (Kingdom Thinking, Missional Engagement and Biblical Community) will determine if we are truly obedient to the command to make disciples. The process of making genuine disciples determines the effectiveness of the church in the West. If we fail to spur on a movement of authentic followers of Jesus who are engaged in His redemptive purposes and instead focus on making converts who turn into consumeristic church attenders needing constant "feeding," we will never see a movement take place.

Now, having emphasized how the three circles relate to the crucial topic of disciple making, let's finish with a brief overview of how the rest of the book is organized.

The four chapters that comprise the "Kingdom Thinking" section will help to recapture a robust Christology that includes not only aspects of the person and work of Jesus, but also the *ways* of Jesus. The person of Jesus stands at the epicenter of who we are and what we do. He must shape everything.

The eight chapters that comprise the "Missional Engagement" section will begin to move people toward practical action steps to better understand and engage a particular context. As we examine the ways of Jesus in the previous section (Christology), this section will inform the purposes of God's people—the church (Missiology). Each chapter builds on the preceding chapter to create continuous momentum for equipping and releasing people into their local mission field. These chapters will help people think and act like a missionary as they follow Jesus into His mission where they live, work and play.

COVOCATIONAL CHURCH PLANTING

A crucial aspect of becoming more like Jesus, and following Him into mission, involves the fourth section of the book, which deals with the concept of biblical community. The chapters in this section will help to recapture the church as a family on mission. If we are not careful, community can become insular. It can become too much about those in the group rather than those outside. It in turn becomes more about safety and comfort instead of about being an agent of God's redemptive mission. The bottom line is that we are created for community. We are designed to be in community with God and with each other. But we must also understand that community can never be fully realized apart from mission.

As a biblical community, we are to be both a foretaste and an instrument of the kingdom. We are a foretaste of the kingdom when the manner in which we live gives the watching world a picture of the kingdom that is to come. We are an instrument of the kingdom as we participate in God's mission. As a community, we strive to discover what God is doing in the lives of people around us, and then discern how He wants us to participant in His redemptive purposes. We must see the church as an instrument, created by God, to be sent into the world to participate in what He is already doing.

The last section of the book is titled "Sustainable Life." The chapters in this section are specifically developed with a church planting leader in mind. We will discuss the unique struggles associated with engaging mission and ministry bivocationally. We want to do everything possible to ensure that while you are planting a church, you also thrive in your family life and vocation.

So, let the journey begin!

ACTION

1. Read this quote from Jurgen Moltmann taken from the book Jesus Christ for Today's World:

   There is no Christology without Christopraxis, no knowledge of Christ without the practice of Christ. We cannot grasp Christ merely with our heads or

> our hearts. We come to understand him through a total, all-embracing practice of living; and that means discipleship...Discipleship is the holistic knowledge of Christ, and for the people involved it has a cognitive as well as an ethical relevance: it means knowing and doing both.[1]

2. Begin a list of activities and/or rhythms in each of the three circles that you and your church plant should consider to both know and do the ways of Jesus. What specific behaviors would develop deeper kingdom thinking? What about in the areas of missional engagement and biblical community?

REFLECTION

1. What thoughts do you have from the Moltmann quote? How have you experienced a deeper understanding of Jesus through the practice of living?
2. What reflections do you have on the disciple-making environment image? Is it a helpful way to think about the key aspects of who we are and what we do as the church?
3. Do you like the concept of apprenticeship to help define discipleship? How might you create an apprenticing process in your church plant?
4. Do you have a plan to disciple people in your church to live on mission? Begin to think what it will look like to create a process to move people from kingdom thinking to missional engagement to biblical community.

SECTION ONE
RETHINK

CHAPTER ONE

RETHINK BIVOCATIONAL CHURCH PLANTING

Believers participate in Christ's priesthood not within the walls of the Church but in the daily business of the world.

— Lesslie Newbigin

RETHINK

Over the past several years there has been an increasing interest in church planting. As a result of declining attendance and the closing of many existing churches, every major denomination is focusing more resources toward starting new congregations. In recent years, we have also seen the creation of multiple church planting networks that emphasize church planting across denominational lines.

In the midst of this proliferation of church planting, one of the most significant trends is the starting of new churches by bivocational leaders. Historically the phrase *bivocational pastor* has been used to refer to a leader who served a church that was unable to compensate a pastor with a full-time salary. Therefore, the pastor would work a second or third job to supplement what the church could provide. In many cases, this was out of necessity rather than preference. Often the language of "tentmaker" (the Apostle Paul's trade described in Acts 18) has been used to define this type of church planter.

However, today there is a new movement among bivocational leaders. More church planters are *choosing* to plant bivocationally. They are making this decision out of the conviction that bivocational church planting actually provides a more desirable way to plant a new church, rather than on the basis of limited funds. In other words, it is becoming a first option, not a last resort.

While there is certainly a place for both bivocational church planting and fully-funded approaches, there are some significant benefits to planting as a bivocational leader. Let's consider three major advantages.

MISSIONAL ENGAGEMENT

Planting as a bivocational leader has significant benefits in that the planter has more opportunities to connect relationally with people in the community. Employment outside the church gives them access to a mission field that is not readily available to a pastor who is employed full time by a local church. Many traditional pastors find themselves working inside a church bubble, spending most of their time talking with church people about things of the church.

Even when a fully-funded pastor makes the effort to engage people in his community, he often finds it challenging to fully relate. Until a person actually incarnates into the local context, he can't begin to understand the values and interests of the people. It is difficult to really love and serve the people God has sent us to from a distance. Some people have referred to this as "marketplace mission" because most of the relationships developed are the result of the planter's vocational connections. His marketplace job isn't a hindrance to what God is doing; it's actually an advantage to engaging in God's mission. Unfortunately, too many Christians don't view vocation in this manner.

COVOCATIONAL CHURCH PLANTING

To illustrate why we need to rethink vocation, let me ask you a question. Think about what you did yesterday. Just take a couple of minutes to think about your day. Now answer this question: What percentage of what you did yesterday was spiritual, and what percentage was secular? Let me ask you a follow-up question. Does selling insurance, running a coffee shop, driving for Uber, teaching at a public school or waiting tables at the local restaurant matter to God?

The point of asking these questions is to illustrate that rethinking vocation must start with considering this sacred-secular divide, or what some people refer to as the problem of dualism. Dualism, simply put, is wrongly dividing something that should not be divided. The Greco-Roman thought was that the world is divided into two competing domains: the sacred (spiritual) and the secular (material). Such a worldview tends to assume that the spiritual is the higher realm, and the secular, or material world, lacks deep meaning. Dualism leads to multiple divisions in thinking, including the division between the clergy (spiritual) and the laity (secular), the church (spiritual) and the world (secular), and between so-called religious practices (Bible study, prayer, worship) and so-called secular practices (work, art, eating).

This form of dualism happens often, and actually becomes harmful to our understanding of bivocational ministry, in our understanding of vocation. The word *vocation* comes from the Latin *vocatio*, meaning a call or summons. It is normally used to refer to a calling or occupation that a person is drawn to or is particularly suited for. The problem of work dualism goes back to the fourth century when Augustine compartmentalized the way people lived when he spoke of the contemplative life and the active life. For Augustine, the contemplative life was given to sacred things and was seen as a higher calling, while the active life was given to secular things and regarded as a lower calling. This kind of thinking helped to create a distorted view of work that continues today.

For example, the words *full-time Christian work* or *full-time ministry* are commonly used to describe those whose vocational calling is to be a pastor, missionary or parachurch worker. However, a proper and biblical understanding is that all Christians are called to full-time ministry, doing good work well for the glory of God, regardless of their specific vocation. If God reigns over all things (and He does), then all things are sacred. But, too often people leave their homes on Monday morning and somehow think they leave God behind. Instead, the church needs to help people recognize that regardless of what God has called them to do, they are contributing to and participating in God's redemptive mission.

The point is that planting a church as a bivocational leader helps to diminish this sacred-secular divide. A congregation sees the church planter model the fact that all vocations are sacred. Regardless of what God has called a person to do, it is a sacred calling. As a result, the benefits of being in the marketplace are multiplied exponentially as every member recognizes how their vocation fits into God's mission.

Further, the sacred-secular divide forces us to reframe how we think about bivocational ministry. In fact, just the term *bivocational* can become a barrier for viewing ministry from a biblical perspective. It invokes the thought of two separate, distinct vocations. We compartmentalize (or bifurcate) seeing little, if any, overlap between what a leader does to earn a living and full-time ministry.

To help overcome this disconnection, I will often use the term *covocation*. The prefix *co* is the reduced form of the Latin *com* which means "together" or "in common." English words like *cofounder*, *copilot*, *coauthor* or *companion* are examples of words that denote partnership and equality. Covocation embodies the reality that if a person is called to be a dentist, a teacher or a plumber, and at the same time is called to start a church, the different callings are not isolated from one another, instead they are actually interlinked and equal. The language of covocation pushes against the temptation to compartmentalize different aspects of our lives. When we begin to understand that each calling is a legitimate and necessary aspect of God's mission, they can be leveraged together for His purposes.

There is, however, a slight distinction that can be made between a bivocational and a covocational church planter. A "bivo" planter is one who has a marketplace job (the tentmaker mentioned earlier) that is viewed as somewhat temporary. The planter's hope is that the church plant will eventually be positioned to provide the financial support for the planter to leave a bivo job to focus full time on the church. A "covo" planter, on the other hand, is one who has a clear and definite calling in the marketplace that they never intend to leave. They know God has called them to be a teacher, mechanic or doctor and they desire to weave that calling into the plan to start a new church.

Another missional benefit of bivocational ministry is that working an occupation in the community builds credibility with those inside and outside the church. In a post-Christian context, where people are skeptical of the church, it is important for non-Chris- tians to see that church leaders have jobs like everyone else. In a time when Christianity doesn't have the best reputation, this can provide significant "street-cred" with those outside the church.

It is important to understand that this new breed of covo planting is missiologically driven. Planters needs to see themselves more as church planting missionaries, than as pastors starting worship services. In other words, planting the church begins by engaging in missionary behaviors. The planter must allow their missiology to inform their ecclesiology, not the other way around. By living like a missionary in a local context, new communities of faith are birthed out of missional engagement.

FINANCIAL STABILITY

A second major benefit of covocational church planting relates to the financial stability it provides in at least three different areas.

THE CHURCH PLANTER

When the primary financial support comes from a marketplace source rather than the church plant, there is usually less financial strain on a family. This is especially true when the planter is employed full time in a vocation that provides benefits like insurance, vacation and retirement.

COVOCATIONAL CHURCH PLANTING

THE NEW CHURCH
A church led by covocational leaders usually has a strong financial base. Without the need to provide full-time salaries and benefits, the church can put more of its financial resources into mission and ministry.

THE CHURCH PLANTING ENTITY
Many denominations have made the commitment to plant hundreds, if not thousands of churches over the next several years. However, there simply aren't enough finances to plant the needed churches with the current funding model. Covocational planting provides the opportunity for funding entities to embrace more sustainable church planting practices. This is especially necessary for planters who are engaging socioeconomically diverse contexts that are made up of the very poor or immigrant populations.

Many traditional church plants start with a large annual budget supported by multiple funding streams, including partnering churches and denominational entities. Because most funding models are structured over a three- to five-year period, the church planter feels pressure to grow the church quickly, so it can become self-sustaining before funding runs out. The unfortunate reality is that a planter is often forced to attract financial givers rather than engaging the brokenness in their community. Covocational church planting, on the other hand, provides a more viable financial model that allows the planter to maintain a clear focus on mission.

SHARED LEADERSHIP
Covocational church planting creates opportunities for leaders in the congregation to use their God-given talents to create a culture of participation rather than one of spectatorship. More church members, out of necessity, become involved in the mission of the church. Covocational leadership helps to diminish the laity-clergy divide. If pastoral leadership is reserved only for the "professionals" then many gifted leaders will miss opportunities to pursue what God has called them to.

COVOCATIONAL CHURCH PLANTING

It is important to understand that bivo and covo church planting is not simply about having two or more jobs; it is really about aligning one life. It's about blending our calling to support our families and ourselves with our calling to live a life engaged in God's mission. We are called to be a missionary people sent into the world to participate in God's redemptive purposes. Planting new communities as bivocational or covocational kingdom leaders is one vital and urgent means to accomplish that task.

I believe there are two major strategies for changing the conversation around this new breed of church planters. First, we need to champion the benefits of bivo and covo church planting, as is laid out in this chapter. But we must also champion the bivo and covo church planters. We need to celebrate the stories of the leaders who have discovered how to leverage their calling in the marketplace along with their calling to plant a new church. Bivo and covo planters, regardless of the size of their church, need to become the new church planting heroes.

Second, I believe to see a church planting movement throughout all walks of life and geographical contexts, we need to create training and resources that are specially tailored for the unique challenges of bivo/covo planting. These resources need to provide a new vision for starting a church from a missiological, grassroots perspective. I hope this book will be a first step in that direction.

If you are already planting a church as a bivo/covo planter, then my prayer is that you would be encouraged as you read this book and that you would grasp more than ever that what you are doing is not only a legitimate church planting approach but *absolutely* necessary.

On the other hand, if you are just beginning to think about bivo/covo church planting, then my prayer for you is that your church planting imagination would be cracked wide open. I pray that you would see the incredible possibilities of starting a new work through your vocation, in your neighborhood or perhaps in some other social space in your community. I pray you would see, maybe for the very first time, that God actually wants to leverage your giftedness in the marketplace for His kingdom purposes.

COVOCATIONAL CHURCH PLANTING

ACTION

1. Articulate the difference between a bivocational and co-vocational church planter.
2. In your own words share the benefits of bivo/covo church planting.

REFLECTION

1. Why is it important to rethink bivocational church planting? Do you find the language of covocational helpful? Why?
2. Can you describe what is meant by the *sacred-secular divide*? Where else do you see this divide played out in Christian culture?

CHAPTER TWO

RETHINK CHURCH AND MISSION

The illiterate of the 21st century will not be those who cannot read and write, but those who cannot learn, unlearn and relearn.

— Alvin Toffler

If mission defines who Christ is, and if Christ sends us as he was sent, then mission defines who we are.

— Albert Curry Winn

RETHINK

When bringing about change in the way people behave, we often need to start with questions of "why" before considering the practical issues of "how." In the book *Start with Why*, author Simon Sinek contends that there are two primary ways to influence human behavior: you can either manipulate it or inspire it. While manipulation is not always negative, for example when a retailer drops the price of a product to motivate a purchase, it unfortunately often involves the use of fear or peer pressure to influence behavior. Additionally, change that is manipulated, is usually short-lived.

Inspiring change, on the other hand, involves the consideration of deeper issues. We need to ask underlying questions of "why." Why do we perceive things in a particular way? Why do we behave in a certain manner? What are the motivations or inherent factors that undergird our behaviors?

Dealing with similar issues of change, author Ronald Heifetz, in his book *Leadership Without Easy Answers*, makes a distinction between organizational change and cultural change. He argues that organizational change typically involves restructuring of some type, along with the use of new programs, processes and techniques. Cultural change, however, looks at how to create a new culture or environment, which will in turn require a completely new set of skills and capacities. Connecting the themes of these two books together, we can say that cultural change is about starting with the why, while organizational change is more about the practical issues of how.

This conversation about change is important in a book about church planting because the answer to the crisis of the church in North America will not be found by making organizational changes. We can't settle with minor adjustments in our ecclesiology or how we do church. Instead, the problem is much more deeply root- ed. We must look to make cultural changes. We must be prepared to ask questions of why. The underlying issues are primarily spiritual, theological and missiological. To plant disciple-making, missional-incarnational churches that have the mindset of reproduction will take deep cultural change in the way we think about God's mission and the nature of the church, as well as how the church engages in that mission in local contexts. We must change our attitude from "we have never done it that way before" to "whatever it takes."

Another way to frame the discussion is to use the language of paradigm. The word *paradigm* is commonly used to refer to a perception, assumption or frame of reference. In the more general sense, it's simply the way we see the world, in terms of perceiving, understanding, and interpreting.

COVOCATIONAL CHURCH PLANTING

Every organization, including the church, is built upon underlying paradigms or assumptions. This is not the same thing as the church's beliefs or theological systems. Rather the paradigm determines how an organization thinks and, therefore, acts. Paradigms explain and then guide behavior. If we try to restructure an organization but leave the original paradigms in place, nothing will change within the organization. Therefore, for real change to take place, we need to experience a paradigm shift or, in most cases, multiple paradigm shifts.

A paradigm shift happens when there is a fundamental change in an underlying assumption. It's a change from one way of thinking to another. There is a transformation, or a sort of metamorphosis that takes place. Now in the context of our understanding of church, mission and church planting, there are at least two reasons we need to experience this type of genuine paradigm shift.

First, those who have been "churched" for a long time typically have some deeply held assumptions about church and mission that may no longer be appropriate in a post-Christendom context. Often these assumptions need to be challenged, or at least investigated, to ensure they are still correct.

Second, cultural change, and ultimately organizational change, will not last if it isn't rooted in paradigm-shift thinking. Without reestablishing certain theological foundations that help us "unlearn and relearn" (to reference the Alvin Toffler quote at the beginning of this chapter), we naturally default toward making modest tweaks in how we operate, rather than cutting to the deeper issues of why. I also believe these theological foundations provide a more robust claim and motivation for real change.

One final thought on the importance of paradigm thinking. An adage that speaks to the importance of considering change in an organization goes like this: We are perfectly designed to achieve what we are currently achieving. Read that again. We are perfectly designed to achieve what we are currently achieving. If we make application of this statement to the church today, one question we might ask would be: Are we satisfied with what we are currently achieving? In other words, are we content or pleased with the impact the church is having today? If we are totally honest, the answer would seem to be a resounding *"No!"*

The fact is, regardless of what marker a person looks at to judge the health of the church in North America, every indicator is trending in the wrong direction. If we are perfectly designed to achieve what the church is currently achieving, then shouldn't we ask if there is an issue in the way we are designed? Or at least question if there is an issue in the way we understand the nature of the church and its place in God's mission? Do we need to reconsider the way we think about church planting? Are there design factors that we need to rethink to achieve the outcomes we desire?

The strategies and techniques that fit previous eras of church history don't seem to work any longer. What we need now is a new set of tools. We need a new vision of reality, a new paradigm—a fundamental change in our thinking that leads to a fundamental change in our behavior, especially as it relates to our understanding of the church and mission.

THE MISSIONARY NATURE OF GOD

The first shift in thinking that must take place relates to our understanding of the missionary nature of God and the church. When we think of the attributes of God, we most often think of characteristics such as holiness, sovereignty, wisdom, justice, love, etc. Rarely do we think of God's missionary nature. But Scripture teaches that God is a missionary God—a sending God.

The missionary nature of God is framed in two primary ways. The first involves the grand narrative of Scripture. When we con- sider the grand story, or meta-narrative of Scripture, we discover it is about God's redemptive purposes. All the great sections of Scripture, all the great stories of the Bible and all the great doctrines of biblical faith coalesce around God's grand plan and purpose for the whole of creation. Mission is the central theme describing God's activity throughout history to restore creation.

A second way to recognize God's missionary nature is to examine the "sending language" used throughout the Bible. From God's sending of Abram in Genesis 12 to the sending of His angel in Revelation 22, there are literally hundreds of examples of sending language that describe God as a missionary-sending God.

In the Old Testament, God is presented as the sovereign Lord who *sends* in order to complete His mission. The Hebrew verb, *shelach* (to send), is found nearly 800 times in the Old Testament. While it is most often used in a variety of non-theological sayings and phrases, it is used more than 200 times with God as the subject of the verb. In other words, it is God who commissions, and it is God who sends.

Perhaps the most dramatic illustration of sending in the Old Testament is found in Isaiah 6. In this passage, we catch a glimpse of God's sending nature in its Trinitarian fullness:

> *"Then I heard the voice of the Lord saying, 'Whom shall I send? And who will go for us?' And I said, 'Here am I! Send me!'" (Isaiah 6:8)*

Later in the book of Isaiah, there is a fascinating passage where the prophet recognizes that God's Spirit has anointed him to "proclaim good news to the poor" and that he is *sent* to "bind up the brokenhearted" (61:1). In the larger passage of Isaiah 61:1-3, it is interesting to note that there are no fewer than six acts of redemption that proceed from, or are dependent upon, the Hebrew verb *sent* or the phrase *he has sent me*. To emphasize how central the sending theme is, the passage could be rendered this way:

> *He has* sent *me, to bind up the brokenhearted,*
> *He has* sent *me, to proclaim freedom for the captives,*
> *He has* sent *me, to release from darkness for the prisoners,*
> *He has* sent *me, to proclaim the year of the Lord's favor and the day of vengeance of our God,*
> *He has* sent *me, to comfort all who mourn,*
> *He has* sent *me, to provide for those who grieve in Zion—*
> *He has* sent *me, to bestow on them a crown of beauty instead of ashes, the oil of joy instead of*

mourning, and a garment of praise instead of a spirit of despair.

Jesus applies this passage to His own ministry in Luke 4:18-19 as He claims to be the human fulfillment of Isaiah 61:1-2. It becomes, in a sense, the closest thing to a personal mission statement for Jesus.

Further, in the prophetic books, it is interesting to note that the Old Testament ends with God promising, through the words of the prophet Malachi, to send a special messenger as the fore-runner of the Messiah: "I will *send* my messenger" (Malachi 3:1). Then the New Testament begins with the arrival of that messenger in the person of John the Baptist, described in the Gospels as a man sent by God (John 1:6).

In the New Testament, sending language is found not only in the Gospels, but also throughout the book of Acts and each of the Epistles. The most comprehensive collection of sending language, however, is found in the Gospel of John, where the words *send* or *sent* are used nearly 60 times. The majority of uses refer to the title of God as "one who sends" and of Jesus as the "one who is sent."

John's Gospel, we see God the Father sending the Son. God the Father and the Son sending the Spirit. And God the Father, Son and Spirit sending the church. In the final climactic-sending passage in John's Gospel, Jesus makes clear that He is not only sent by the Father, but now He is the sender, as He sends the disciples: "As the Father has sent me, I am sending you" (John 20:21).

With this sentence, Jesus is doing much more than drawing a vague parallel between His mission and ours. Deliberately and precisely, He is making His mission the model for ours. Our understanding of the church's mission must flow from our understanding of Jesus' mission as revealed in the Gospels.

THE MISSIONARY NATURE OF THE CHURCH

But why does it matter that we recognize God's mission as the grand narrative of Scripture? Why is it important to see the "sending language" throughout every book of the Bible? Here is why. *The nature and essence of the church is rooted in the missionary nature of God.* In other words, if God is a missionary God (and He is!), then we as His people are missionary people. Therefore, the church doesn't just *send* missionaries; the church *is* the missionary.

Individually and collectively as the body of Christ, we are a sent, missionary church. We should be sending the people in the church out among the people of the world rather than attempting to at- tract the people of the world in among the people of the church. But a major problem in the life of the church in North America is that the vast majority of people in the church today do not think of their congregation in a sending, missionary manner. Instead, most people today understand the church in two prominent ways.

REFORMATION VIEW

The first view is what some call the "Reformation" perspective.[2] The point with this understanding of the church is that Protestants have inherited a particular view of church from the Reformers, which emphasizes the right preaching of the Word, the right administration of the ordinances and the proper exercise of church discipline. Historically these three activities have been referred to as the "marks" of the church.

While each of the three marks are important aspects of church life, this view has left us with an understanding of the church as a *place where certain things happen.* In other words, a person *goes to* church to hear the Bible taught correctly, to participate in the Lord's Supper and baptism and, in some cases, to experience church discipline. Once again, all very good things, but is that the way we want to define the church? Does a *place-where-certain-things-happen* understanding speak to the real essence and nature of the church?

CONTEMPORARY VIEW

The second view is a slight variation on the Reformation definition. This contemporary view is perhaps the most prevalent way people in America understand the church today—that it is a *vendor of religious goods and services.* From this perspective, members are viewed as customers for whom religious goods and services are produced. Churchgoers expect the church to provide a wide range of religious services, such as great worship music, preaching, children's programs, small groups, parenting seminars and so on.

One of the major issues with these views of defining the church is that the church is seen as an institution that exists for the benefit of its members.

The alternative vision of the church is to see it as a people *called* and *sent* by God to participate in His redemptive mission for the world. The nature of the church—rooted in the very nature of God—is missionary. Rather than seeing ourselves primarily as a *sending* body, we must see ourselves as a body that is *sent*. Of course, the church still gathers, but the difference is that we don't simply gather for our own sake, but instead for the sake of others—or better yet, for the sake of God's mission. We come together as a collective body of followers of Jesus to be equipped through prayer, worship and study and then to be *sent* out into the world. The church is to be a gathered *and* scattered people. Missionary Lesslie Newbigin stated it this way:

> *The church is the bearer to all the nations of a gospel that announces the kingdom, the reign, and the sovereignty of God ... It is not meant to call men and women out of the world into a safe religious enclave but to call them out in order to send them back as agents of God's kingship.*

PARTICIPATION IN THE MISSIO DEI

But practically speaking, what does it look like to be agents of God's kingship? How do we engage in mission alongside what God is already doing? The answer, at least in part, involves the concept of *missio Dei*. An English rendering of this Latin phrase speaks to the "mission of God." It states that it is God who has a mission to set things right in a broken world—to redeem and restore it to what He has always intended.

Therefore, mission is not the invention, responsibility or program of the church. Instead, it flows directly from the character and purposes of a missionary God. In the words of South African missiologist David Bosch, "It is not the church which undertakes mission; it is the *missio Dei* which constitutes the church." Or stated in a slightly different way, "It is not so much that God has a mission for His church in the world, but that God has a church for His mission in the world."[3]

It is not only crucial to understand that God has a mission, it is equally important to understand that His mission is larger than the church. We in the church often wrongly assume that the *primary* activity of God is in the church, rather than recognizing that God's primary activity is in the world, and the church is God's instrument *sent* into the world to participate in His redemptive mission. Instead of thinking of the church as an entity that simply *sends* missionaries, we instead need to view the church *as* the missionary. Among other things, this shift in perspective will bring about radical changes in two specific areas.

GOD'S MISSION AS THE ORGANIZING PRINCIPLE

First a *missio Dei* perspective will shape our thinking about the form and function of the church. Typically, congregations view "missions" as simply one program or activity among many other equally important functions of the church. Therefore, the missions program is seen alongside that of worship, small groups, men's and women's ministries, youth and children's ministry, etc.

However, when the church begins to define itself as an agent of God's mission, it will begin to organize *every* activity of the church around the *missio Dei*. Mission as the organizing principle means that mission goes way beyond being some sort of optional activity or program of the church. It actually is the organizing axis of the church. The life of the church will focus on and revolve around God's mission. Now this does not minimize the other activities of the church, such as teaching, corporate worship and community. But it does mean the other activities are catalyzed by and organized around the mission function.

GOD'S MISSION AS THE STARTING POINT

The second way a *missio Dei* perspective will change how we think of mission has to do with where we start. In other words, if it is re- ally about what God is doing, then we must look for God's activity in a local setting as the place to begin our missional engagement.

This is vitally important for the church planting process. Instead of "front loading" mission strategies with what we *think* a community needs, we begin by listening and learning what God is already doing. Only after discovering what God is up to in a particular setting do we then ask how He wants us to participate. A *missio Dei* theology should challenge a church planter to think less like a pastor who is starting a Sunday worship service and more like a church planting missionary who has been sent to a local setting.

One practical way to frame this type of participation in God's mission is to consider the "Three Ds" of missional engagement.

DISCOVER

If it is truly God's mission and not ours, then we must first discover how God is at work. The first step is listening. Individually and collectively, we must cultivate our ability to listen well on three fronts: to the Spirit, the local community and to each other. It is simply impossible to ascertain the movement of God without carving out significant time to listen to His voice through prayer and Scripture, as well as the voices of those whom we desire to serve. If the first step is about discovering, then the first question has to be, "What is God doing in this place?"

DISCERN

In addition to listening, participating in God's mission will involve the difficult task of discernment. Not only will we need to discern what God is already doing, but we will need to ask the follow-up question, "In light of my (our) gifts and resources, how does God want me to participate in what He is doing?" The fact is we can't do it all, which is true for both individual followers of Jesus and local congregations. But it is also true that God has gifted us all to do something! The point of discernment is to determine where and how to participate in God's mission.

DEBRIEF
Throughout the process of engaging God's mission, we must create opportunities to reflect on our missional involvement. Sometimes this may simply mean we need individual down time to reflect upon our activities. We may need to ask God to affirm our involvement or to ask for clarity of direction. But it will also mean carving out time to reflect with others within our faith community. We need to hear what others are seeing and sensing concerning God's activities and to hear the stories of how others are engaging God's mission. It is important for us to be in position to offer feedback on what we are sensing.

These "Three Ds" hopefully help to focus the emphasis on the context to which God has sent us, but they should also remind us that He has already been working in that place long before we ever arrived.

ACTION

1. Identify at least two people groups or geographical locations in your city or neighborhood to which God is looking to send someone.
2. List areas in your life that may need to change for *you* to be able to say, "Here am I. Send me!" What is the first step you will take to overcome each hindrance?
3. Identify at least two people groups or geographical locations in your city to which God is looking to send your church plant.
4. List areas in the life of your church that may need to change for the church to be able to say "Here are we. Send us!" What is the first step your church might take to overcome each hindrance?

REFLECTION

1. What reflections do you have on the missionary nature of God?
2. How does this chapter influence the way you think about your own life?
3. What thoughts do you have on the different views of the church? Which of the views describes your perspective of the church best? What about your church planting team?
4. Can you give examples of how you or your church has "front-loaded" missions?

SECTION TWO

KINGDOM THINKING (CHRISTOLOGY)

CHAPTER THREE

RECALIBRATING BACK TO JESUS

The whole life of Jesus is to be understood as determinative for the life of the church.

— Stanley Hauerwas

The center and foundation of Christian faith is Jesus of Nazareth, the Messiah, crucified and risen, and present with us now in the power of the Spirit.

— Harold Wells

The ultimate problem, which has caused our theological help- lessness, lies in the separation between Jesus Christ and the Church.

— Dietrich Ritschl

RETHINK

As stated in the introduction, our Christology (*Kingdom Thinking*) should determine our missiology (*Missional Engagement*), which in turn should determine our ecclesiology (*Biblical Community*). When we get these three concepts in the wrong order, we often allow our idea of church to govern our sense of purpose and mission.

As a result, we spend too much time discussing the forms of worship, church structure and types of programs and fail to recognize that our ecclesiology flows more naturally out of a deep sense of mission. Jesus determines our purpose and mission in the world, and then our mission to follow Him should drive us to discover different approaches of being the church. Bottom line—we must start with Jesus!

However, we not only need to *start* with Jesus (Christology), individually and as the body of Christ, but we must recalibrate *back* to Jesus on a regular basis. Discipleship at its basic core is becoming more and more like Jesus and experiencing His life as it is lived through us. The act of disciple making lies at the center of our task as the church. At its very heart, Christianity is a Jesus movement, one that seeks to consistently embody the life, teachings and mission of its founder. In its utter simplicity, Christianity is *all* about Jesus. Therefore, we must constantly go back to Jesus. How did He live? What did He do? What were His primary teachings and rhythms of life? With whom did He spend time? All of this means that recovery of the centrality of Jesus (Christology) is the key to the renewal of the church as it defines who we are and what we do.

But practically speaking, what does it look like to recalibrate back to Jesus? How can we once again be shaped by every aspect of the life of Jesus? At least part of the answer lies in the need to cultivate a robust Christology.

CULTIVATING A ROBUST CHRISTOLOGY

The word *Christology* comes from two Greek words meaning *Christ* and *study*. When combined, the word means *the study of Christ*. Typically, the word *Christology* is used to refer to the study of the *person* and *work* of Jesus. In other words, *who* was Jesus and what did He *do*—particularly on the cross? However, when using the word *robust* to describe a certain view of Christology, I am simply arguing for a more comprehensive examination of the person, work and *ways* of Jesus. That is, what aspects of the life of Jesus have we missed or, at times, minimized? If Jesus is the Alpha and Omega (Revelation 1:8; 21:6; 22:13) and the founder and perfecter of our faith (Hebrews 12:2), then we must ensure we have a broad view of the entire Jesus event.

Below is an image to illustrate a comprehensive view of Christology. You will notice the centrality of the cross in the middle of the image. We *cannot* minimize Jesus' atoning work on the cross. However, there are other aspects of the life of Jesus that have profound implications on the development of our missiology (Missional Engagement) and our ecclesiology (Biblical Community). While the limitations of this chapter will not allow unpacking every aspect of the image, let's consider a couple of key elements.

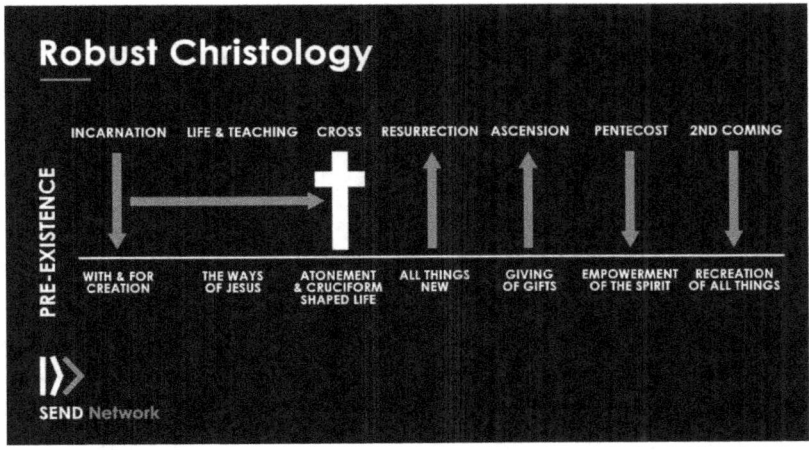

One of the most profound aspects of Christology that is often diminished is the Incarnation of Jesus. The lack of attention on this aspect of the life of Jesus has affected the way we think of missiology. The Incarnation of Jesus should inform our posture toward our context. It should shape the way we think about and do mission.

The word *incarnation* comes from a Latin word that literally means *in the flesh*. It refers to the act whereby God took on human flesh and entered our world to bring about reconciliation between Himself and humanity. The Incarnation is God's ultimate missional participation in creation (John 3:16-17).[4] When God entered our world in and through the person of Jesus, He came to live among us (*eskenosen*—literally, "set up a tent"): "The Word became flesh and blood, and moved into the neighborhood" (John 1:14, The Message).

The Incarnation qualifies God's acts in the world and must also qualify ours. If God's central way of reaching His world was to incarnate Himself in Jesus, then our way of reaching the world should likewise be incarnational. Now it is important to recognize that the Incarnation of Jesus was a special, unrepeatable event. Further, as we enter the world of others, we certainly cannot take on another's identity in the fully integrated way that Jesus did. But we can make a distinction between *the* Incarnation with a capital "I" and incarnational mission.

When we seriously consider the Incarnation as part of a robust Christology, we begin to allow it to significantly influence how we live. We begin to understand that in the Incarnation of Jesus, God revealed something about Himself—that He is *with* and *for* creation. Read that sentence again. In the Incarnation of Jesus, we learn that God is *with* and *for* creation.

And now as the risen Jesus (resurrection and ascension) sends His Spirit (Pentecost) to empower the church, we are to be *with* and *for* the world. The Incarnation illustrates for us that God, through Christ, is our advocate. And now we are to be an advocate for the world. We are to an advocate for the sinner. Unfortunately, when we don't allow the Incarnation of Jesus to inform our posture toward the culture, we end up being an adversary to the other rather than an advocate.

Another aspect of a robust Christology involves the life and teaching of Jesus, or the *ways* of Jesus. There are significant missional implications in the way Jesus did life with others. We, too, often forget the radical nature of Jesus' relationships. Religious insiders challenged Him not because of His doctrine but because of those to whom He extended God's gracious and loving hospitality. As we will discuss in future chapters, as followers of Jesus we are called to cross society's boundaries, to eat as Jesus ate, to be a people of open- ness and acceptance, of gratitude and generosity.[5]

As Rodney Clapp has observed,

> *Jesus spoke parables honoring such despised ethnic groups as Samaritans, thereby ignoring racial boundaries. He scandalously taught women and conversed with them in public, thereby trespassing sexual borders. He included among his disciples Simon the Zealot and spoke the words of new life to Nicodemus the Pharisee, thereby opening himself to the array of people who were strangers to one another by virtue of their politics. He called the adulteress from the estrangement of the stoning circle back into the circle of community, thereby crossing moral borders. And he invited the ritually "unclean" to his table, thereby breaking religious taboos.[6]*

We often miss this radical aspect of Jesus' relationships because we know Jesus as Lord and Savior (cross and resurrection), but sometimes forget He is also our guide and example.

How then do we begin a move toward being influenced, both personally and as a church, by the ways of Jesus? Among other things, it will mean taking the Gospels seriously as the primary texts that define us as Jesus people. It will mean acting like Jesus in relation to people outside the faith. It will mean asking probing questions (see the reflection section) that challenge our often-reduced view of Christology. In turn, we will discover that the chief solution to our sometimes inadequate view of missiology and ecclesiology is more Jesus.

In the book *ReJesus: A Wild Messiah for a Missional Church*, the authors offer a fitting metaphor for recalibrating to Jesus.

> *Throughout the Apollo missions to the moon, spacecraft regularly drifted off course. In fact, more than 80 percent of their journey through space was slightly off course. To conserve fuel, the spaceships drift through space, moved by the gravitational pull of the earth. Jet engines are*

> used occasionally only when the ship is getting too far off course to readjust their coordinates and get them back on track. The occasional burst of their massive engines completes the readjustment and keeps them heading toward their destination. We think this is a useful metaphor for the church today. Many people are claiming that the church has been drifting off course and needs a burst of renewed power to get back on track. However, for spacecraft, that surge of propulsion works only if the coordinates are accurate and the flight plan is properly conceived. Today, many voices are calling the church back on track, acting like power surges for a drifting church. But our contention is that the church needs to go back to the drawing board and work again on its flight plan. If the plan is wrong, all the bursts of renewed energy will only push us further into space.[7]

The only legitimate and accurate flight plan is Jesus. If we truly de- sire for our church planting efforts to experience kingdom impact then we must constantly recalibrate back to the person, work and ways of Jesus.

ACTION

1. Study the Gospels. Read and reread the four Gospels. Develop a habit of marinating your mind and soul in the Gospels. Perhaps set up a community rhythm where everyone reads the same Gospel in the same time period. Or assign a Gospel per month that everyone reads together. Consider exploring the parables that Jesus told and seek to integrate the truths into everyday life. Explore what Jesus said about certain themes such as the kingdom of God, prayer, money or possessions.

2. Read about Jesus. Choose a book written about Jesus that everyone who is part of your church planting team or missional community can read together.
3. Take a few minutes to examine the "Robust Christology" image. As you consider each aspect of the image, write down how they could influence the way you think about and engage in God's mission.

REFLECTION

Answer the following questions yourself; then ask these same questions of those in your planting team or missional community:
1. What ongoing role does Jesus play in shaping the content and culture of the church?
2. How is the Christian religion informed and shaped by the Jesus we meet in the Gospels?
3. How do you assess the consistency or inconsistency between the life and example of Jesus and the current form of Christianity?
4. How can you best recalibrate back to Jesus? How can that recalibration renew your discipleship, Christian community and the ongoing mission of the church?

CHAPTER FOUR

THE GOSPEL OF THE KINGDOM

Seek first the kingdom of God.

– Jesus

The kingdom of God is what the world looks like when King Jesus gets His way.

– Jeff Christopherson

RETHINK

In the past several years, there has been a significant focus on the gospel and the idea of "gospel-centered" ministry. This shift has been a needed recalibration back to the biblical text and our understanding of the person and work of Jesus. However, we need to ensure there is clarity in what is meant when someone uses the word *gospel*. When we talk about the gospel, are we speaking in a way that is consistent with the story of Jesus and the message of the early church?

In the foreword to Scot McKnight's excellent book, *King Jesus Gospel*, N.T. Wright states:

> *For many people, "the gospel" has shrunk right down to a statement about Jesus' death ... and a*

> *prayer with which people accept it. That matters the way the rotor blades of a helicopter matter. You won't get off the ground without them. But rotor blades alone don't make a helicopter. And a micro-cosmic theory of atonement and faith don't, by themselves, make up "the gospel."*[8]

How then are we to understand the gospel? Let's start with the term *gospel*. In the New Testament, the word for gospel is the word *euangelion*. It has the prefix *eu*, which means *good* or *pleasant*. The word *angelos* or *angelion* is the word for *message*. Therefore, in its most basic sense the word *gospel*, or *euangelion*, means *good message* or *good news*.

In the New Testament, we find three ways in which the word *gospel* is used. First, we have the four books in the New Testament that are called the Gospels of Matthew, Mark, Luke and John. These books are biographical stories of the person of Jesus.

Second, during the early ministry of Jesus, the word *gospel* was linked not so much with the person of Jesus but with the theme of the kingdom of heaven. For example, John the Baptist is introduced in the book of Matthew as one who comes "preaching the gospel," with a message to "repent, for the kingdom of heaven is at hand" (Matthew 3:2, ESV). Jesus also spoke often about the kingdom. The phrase, "kingdom of God" or "kingdom of heaven" occurs more than 100 times in the Gospels; 89 of those are in Matthew and Luke alone. Clearly for Jesus, the good news was the good news of the kingdom.

Third, in the Epistles the term *gospel* takes on a nuance of understanding. It became the gospel *about* Jesus. At the heart of this gospel was the announcement of who Jesus was and what He had accomplished in His lifetime. There was a definite content to the gospel. The apostle Paul states in 1 Corinthians:

> *Now I would remind you, brothers, of the gospel I preached to you, which you received, in which you stand, and by which you are being saved, if you hold fast to the word I preached to you— unless you believed in vain. For I delivered to you*

> as of first importance what I also received: that Christ died for our sins in accordance with the Scriptures, that he was buried, that he was raised on the third day in accordance with the Scriptures, and that he appeared to Cephas, then to the twelve (15:1-5, ESV).

This passage reads like a plot summary of the passion narrative found in each of the four Gospels. Its emphasis is on events—Jesus' death, resurrection and appearances. These events form the core of what Paul called the "gospel I preached to you." However, we need to recognize that while the event of Jesus' death is most *certainly* linked to the doctrine of sin and atonement, the theological significance of His death is rooted in the overarching historical events of the whole life of Jesus.

This is true throughout the Epistles, where the good news is about Jesus' life of perfect obedience, His atoning death on the cross, His resurrection, His ascension and His outpouring of the Holy Spirit upon the church. In this way, the gospel is seen as more than a set of doctrines. It is a person. The central affirmation of the early church was that Jesus was the Messiah. Jesus was the King. Jesus was the Lord. The gospel for the early church was to tell the whole Jesus story. They saw evangelism as the announcement of an event, the description of a salvation-bringing event in history. They were more concerned with announcing the Jesus event than they were with detailed descriptions of doctrinal belief.

In the book *Kingdom First*, author Jeff Christopherson challenges us to make a clear distinction:

> *Do you worship a set of truths that make up what you con- sider to be the gospel, or do you worship Jesus, the person about whom those truths speak? It may appear to be splitting hairs at first, but it is a distinction you cannot miss. One is a journey to life; the other is a cold and ominous path to death. Bring people to Jesus, not precepts about Jesus. Communicate Jesus the person rather than a set of statements as if you are convincing people to change their views on*

> politics. He is the Messiah whom the Old Testament anticipated and whom the New Testament celebrated. If we are going to offer good news, rather than simply winning sacred arguments or changing people's moral positions, we must bring people to the ultimate good news: the person of Jesus Christ.[9]

JESUS AND THE KINGDOM OF GOD

If Jesus is the gospel, then it is incumbent upon us to discover how He communicated the good news. As mentioned earlier, for Jesus, the "kingdom of God" (or "kingdom of heaven") was His favorite way of talking about the gospel. The language is unmistakable throughout the Gospels: "The kingdom of heaven is like this," "The kingdom of heaven is within you," "The kingdom of God has come near," "until the kingdom of God comes," "I must preach the kingdom of God."

To fully comprehend the story of Jesus, we must see how His death and resurrection relate to His kingdom agenda as presented in the Gospels. We simply can't understand one without the other. But how are we to grasp the way Jesus spoke of the kingdom? A good place to start is to understand that the word *kingdom* is a combination of two words: *king* and *domain*. It refers to the realm of a king's dominion, including his laws, codes and commands. Citizens in a kingdom must abide by the decrees of their king and give him their total allegiance. And they are not to follow or obey any rival ruler who would seek to take any of the authority away from the reigning king.[10] To do so would be treason. A kingdom refers to the king's reign, where what the king wants done, gets done.

Now for our purposes, let's understand the kingdom of God to be God's active reign through history bringing about His purposes in the world through Jesus. In the simplest of terms, *the kingdom of God is what the world looks like when King Jesus gets His way.*

Once again from *Kingdom First*:

> Although brokenness abounds within individuals, institutions, and structural systems, there is good news. Jesus, our triumphant King, wants things

> to be much different in our damaged world. He desires to bring the peace of His atonement and His eternal victory into all the manifestations of brokenness in our world (according to Col. 1:19–20). While we now live in the tension that we will not wholly see the fullness of Christ's peace until the new heaven and the new earth, there is a promise of peace where sorrow currently abounds. This is the gospel of the Kingdom.... According to Jesus, who is the Gospel, He Himself pro- claimed the good news, liberated captives, healed the sick, freed the oppressed, and brought the Lord's favor to the least. All of this was Jesus' activity on this earth and His fulfillment of Isaiah's prophesy. This work of our King is what brings the Kingdom of God to the dark and broken realities of a desperate world. Peace where there was chaos. Healing where there was pain. Comfort where there was deep sorrow. Wholeness where there was systemic fragmentation.[11]

Another aspect of Jesus' message we must realize is that the kingdom of God is not something we *build* or *expand*. These two verbs are not found in the New Testament's language for the kingdom of God. The announcement of God's kingdom or reign nowhere includes an invitation to go out and build it or to expand it.

Instead, the kingdom is something we *enter*. We *receive* it. These words, which are often intertwined in a passage of Scripture, suggest a very different missional engagement. "Truly I tell you, whoever does not *receive* the kingdom of God as a little child will never *enter* it" (Luke 18:17, NRSV). In that same context, Jesus notes how hard it is for those who have riches to *enter* the reign, or kingdom of God (vv. 24-25). Because it is God's realm, and not ours, we *enter* the kingdom; we do not, and cannot, build it.

Moreover, the *only* entrance into His kingdom is obedience to the work, words and ways of Jesus. He is *the* way. If we hope to experience God's peace, we commit to becoming peacemakers. If we desire to inherit the earth, we stop fighting for it. We commit to meekness rather than the use of power. If we want to live in the realm of God's mercy, we become practitioners of mercy in our attitudes and actions.

THE KINGDOM OF GOD AS MISSIONAL PERSPECTIVE

It is important to get this message of the kingdom right because it has significant implications on the way we understand mission and evangelism. This discussion is an excellent example of how our Christology shapes or determines our missiology. The language of *entering* or *receiving* provides a humble starting point for mission. It is in stark contrast to a more activist notion of building or ex- tending the kingdom. Instead, we are entering into the work of the King. We are following King Jesus into His mission of redemption. As we follow Him there will no doubt be battles with powers and principalities as we work to restore that which is broken in our cities, but we must remember that we are partnering with Him. We are participating in what He is already doing. The way in which we see Jesus doing His work influences the way we do our work.

Further, the language of receiving the reign or kingdom of God should help shape our view of personal discipleship. Daily life becomes a discipline of asking how we may move more squarely into the realm of God's kingdom. How can we live more obediently to His reign? How can we welcome and receive it into the fabric of our lives? And how do we recognize and better engage in His kingdom activity?

Lastly, a kingdom of God perspective provides a much more welcoming framework for evangelism. Missiologist Lois Barrett shares how an understanding of the reign of God should influence the church's posture toward those outside the church:

> *Evangelism would move from an act of recruiting or co-opting those outside the church to an invitation of companionship. The church would witness that its members, like others, hunger for the hope that there is a God who reigns in love and intends the good of the whole earth. The community of the church would testify that they*

> have heard the announcement that such a reign is coming, and indeed is already breaking into the world. They would confirm that they have heard the open welcome and received it daily, and they would invite others to join them as those who also have been extended God's welcome. To those invited, the church would offer itself to assist their entrance into the reign of God and to travel with them as co-pilgrims.[12]

Back to the original discussion at the beginning of this chapter. What is the gospel or good news? It is not primarily about where will we go when we die. The good news is found in the person of Jesus. And the message of good news that Jesus proclaimed is that the kingdom of God, the sovereign rule of God, is breaking into the present world. Further, the work and ways of Jesus (His incarnation, death, resurrection, ascension and gift of the Spirit) are de- signed not to take us away from this earth but rather to make us agents of the transformation of this earth.

God did not want to rescue humans from creation any more than he wanted to rescue Israel from the Gentiles. "He wanted to rescue Israel in order that Israel might be a light to the Gentiles, and He wanted thereby to rescue humans in order that humans might be His rescuing stewards over creation."[13] Which, of course, only takes place through the cross. That is the inner dynamic of the kingdom of God.

ACTION

1. Articulate in your own words the meaning of the word *gospel*. How would you define the kingdom?

REFLECTION

1. How has this chapter challenged your view of the gospel? What about the kingdom of God?

2. How does the contrast in language from "expand" and "build" to "enter" and "receive" change your view of the kingdom? What are some personal implications of that change?

CHAPTER FIVE

THE KINGDOM AGENDA

It is a terrible misunderstanding of the Gospel to think that it offers us salvation while relieving us of responsibility for the life of the world, for the sin and sorrow and pain with which our human life and that of our fellow men and women is so deeply interwoven.

— Lesslie Newbigin

Despite what people think, within the Christian family and out- side it, the point of Christianity isn't "to go to heaven when you die."

— N. T. Wright

While we believe in Jesus as Savior of the private soul, we remain largely unconvinced about His ideas for saving the world.

— Brian Zahnd

RETHINK

In the last chapter, we discussed how the kingdom of God was central to the teachings of Jesus. Proclaiming the good news of the kingdom was His primary message and mission. The message of the kingdom is good news because it is about God's active reign through history to bring about His purposes in the world through Jesus. In the simplest of terms, *the kingdom of God is what the world looks like when King Jesus gets His way*. But how does the church fit into the concept of the kingdom? What role does the church play in Jesus' kingdom agenda?

Unfortunately, in North America, Christianity is viewed (by both those inside and outside the church) largely as a church-centered practice; it is a religious organization that exists for Christians. This "prevailing perspective in far too many congregations is a misguided view of the nature and role of the church in God's mission. Not only is it unbiblical, but it also undermines, distorts, and discredits God's Kingdom agenda."[14]

As stated earlier, the church cannot create or build the kingdom, but it can witness to it. This witness happens in word and deed, in miracles, in the transformation of the lives of people, in the presence of the Holy Spirit and in the radical recreation of humanity. A local congregation's witness to the rule of the King is itself part of the content of the kingdom of God which is proclaimed. The kingdom comes as Jesus is made known. Local congregations participate in the coming of the kingdom as they live out their lives as biblical communities made up of disciples of the King. They become branch offices of the kingdom.[15]

We simply cannot fully understand the scope and depth of the congregation's mission unless we see it in relation to the kingdom of God in the world. The church must embrace and embody a new narrative that is motivated by God's mission and kingdom concerns rather than church issues.

In the book *Kingdom Come*, author Reggie McNeal shares an illustration that helps to clarify the distinction between kingdom and church.

> *An airport is not designed to be a destination. No one plans a vacation to hang out at the airport or to take in the sights at their nearest transportation hub. In fact, when people have to spend more*

> time at the airport than they planned, they usually aren't happy about it. The airport's job is to get people to somewhere else as quickly and efficiently as possible. That doesn't mean the airport is unimportant—not at all! In fact, a properly functioning airport is crucial to the journey's success. But the airport is not the point of the trip. The airport is not the destination. And no airport can hold a candle to the destination that prompted the journey in the first place. I'm sure you can see where this is going. The church is not the destination, and it's not the point of the journey. It's the life of the Kingdom that we're trying to get to. That's what people are after. That's what the trip is all about. When we keep people hanging around at the church too long, we're taking them off-mission and messing up their journey.[16]

Now this doesn't mean the church is unimportant. In fact, it is vitally important! A properly functioning church is crucial for people to enter and participate in the kingdom. But the church is not a substitute for the kingdom.

So, what role does the church play in the kingdom agenda? What does it mean for the church to embrace kingdom concerns? How are we to best understand what it looks like to have local congregations participate in the coming kingdom?

Missiologist Lesslie Newbigin, who was a British missionary to India, provides a helpful way to think about the church's relationship to the kingdom when he states that the church lives as a sign, foretaste and instrument of the kingdom of God.[17] The church finds its identity and mission in what it points to as a *sign*, what it tastes like as a *foretaste* and what it participates in bringing about as an *instrument*. All three of these terms are closely linked to the mission of the church. Let's briefly examine each of these ideas.

THE CHURCH AS A SIGN OF THE KINGDOM

The purpose of a sign is to point to something not yet fully visible—pointing people to a reality that is right around the corner. The church is described as the sign of God's wisdom in Ephesians: "so that through the church the manifold wisdom of God might now be made known to the rulers and authorities in the heavenly places" (3:10, ESV). Our way of life together as the church ought to point people to God's future.

THE CHURCH AS A FORETASTE OF THE KINGDOM

The church serves as a foretaste when people get a taste of God's future in the present. The church is a foretaste when it demonstrates what life is like when men and women live under the rule and reign of God. The church shows the world what it means to embody forgiveness and live in harmony and love with one another. In this way, the church becomes a tangible, though not perfect, foretaste of the kingdom that is to come. "The church ought to be a tangible appetizer of God's future."[18]

Author Michael Frost uses the analogy of a movie trailer to explain what it means for the church to be a foretaste. When people go to see a film, usually a series of trailers or previews from upcoming releases are shown before the main attraction. Frost says this about those previews:

> *Trailers are tasters, short film versions of the soon-to-be-released feature, and they usually include the best special effects or the funniest scenes or the most romantic moments, depending on the film, of the forthcoming feature. Now, watch those around you in the theatre at the end of each trailer. If it has done its job, usually one person will turn to the other and say, "I want to see that movie."*
>
> *This is a great metaphor for the missional church. If it does its job well, people will see what it does*

> and say, "I want to see the world they come from." Far from being a cute illustration, this is at the very core of Christian mission. The church is to be like a trailer for the New Jerusalem, a taster, with all the best bits on full display. If we conclude that the world to come will be a place of complete and perfect justice, it follows that the mission of the church is to create foretastes of the justice to come.
>
> Likewise, if we believe that the world to come is a place of love and mercy, we are to be a trailer of that love and mercy, a free sample for those looking to buy into the whole thing. Read the Scriptures and compile a picture of the world to come—justice, love, peace, reconciliation—and then go forth to fashion foretastes of that world. But, of course, if we believe that in the New Jerusalem "every knee should bow...and every tongue confess that Jesus Christ is Lord" (Philippians 2:10–11), our mission is to create foretastes of such worship by encouraging belief where there is currently unbelief. In this way we both demonstrate and announce the reign of God through Christ.[19]

Thinking of the church as a foretaste should inspire the church to live a countercultural life that is in stark contrast to the ways of the world. Jesus calls us to a radically different way of life as a foretaste of the kingdom. It is a call to be people of blessing; to live lives of generosity and grace, service and hospitality. To be beautiful examples of reconciliation, joy and contentment in a culture full of division, negativity and anxiety.

THE CHURCH AS AN INSTRUMENT OF THE KINGDOM

As stated in the airport illustration, the church is not the final destination. Instead, local churches are instruments of something much greater than themselves. They are tools of the kingdom of

God. We in the church often wrongly assume that the *primary* activity of God is in the church, rather than recognizing that God's primary activity is in the world, and the church is God's instrument *sent* into the world to participate in His kingdom mission of redemption. It is interesting to note that being an instrument of the kingdom represents an active role. In other words, we are actively discovering ways to join the kingdom agenda. We are constantly looking for ways to participate in God's mission. For this reason, Paul can address Christians as "co-workers for the kingdom of God" (Colossians 4:11) and consider them to be "suffering" for the reign of God (2 Thessalonians 1:5).

It is also good to recognize that we are instruments in both word *and* deed. In word, we are messengers of the kingdom. We proclaim the good news of God's rule and reign in Christ. But as messengers, we also bring those words to life in tangible ways. We will announce (heralding, worship, evangelism), and we will demonstrate (justice, love, reconciliation) that reign.

When considering the importance of demonstration, it is helpful to be reminded that in Scripture there are more than 2,000 passages that express God's heart for the vulnerable and weak. Not only do these texts show us that God cares for people in their dis- tress, but He expects us—as His body—to have the same concern.

For instance, Deuteronomy 10:18 says, "He executes justice for the orphan and the widow, and shows His love for the alien by giving him food and clothing." In Zechariah 7:9-10, we read, "Dispense true justice and practice kindness and compassion…and do not oppress the widow or the orphan, the stranger or the poor." Also, Psalm 68:5 says that God is a "father to the fatherless, a defender of widows." Throughout the Old Testament, we see these teachings again and again.

The New Testament continues this same storyline of examples among God's people and calls from the Lord to engage in issues of justice. Approximately one-third of passages in the four gospels record Jesus' acts of justice and mercy. In the book of Acts, we see the church caring for the physical needs of other members: "There was not a needy person among them, for as many as were owners of lands or houses sold them and brought the proceeds of what was sold and laid it at the apostles' feet, and it was distributed to each as any had need" (Acts 4:34-35). In 2 Corinthians 9:7-15, Paul teaches us that we are blessed so that we will abound in good works, scattering gifts to the poor and bringing about righteousness that endures forever. Illustrated in numerous New Testament passages, the church is called to *demonstrate* peace and healing to a broken world. (See Matthew 5:3; 6:2-3; 19:21; 25:34-40; Mark 12:42-43; 14:7; Luke 4:18; 12:33; 14:13-14; 19:22; Acts 9:36; 10:31; 24:17; Romans 15:26; 1 Corinthians 13:3; Galatians 2:10; 1 Timothy 5:3-4; 5:16; James 1:27; 2:1-6.)

CONCLUSION

The language of kingdom often evokes images of powerful empires, mighty armies and noble families. But that is not the image Jesus presented of the kingdom of God.

> *He said therefore, "What is the kingdom of God like? And to what shall I compare it? It is like a grain of mustard seed that a man took and sowed in his garden, and it grew and became a tree, and the birds of the air made nests in its branches."*
>
> *And again he said, "To what shall I compare the kingdom of God? It is like leaven that a woman took and hid in three measures of flour, until it was all leavened." (Luke 13:18-21, ESV)*

Jesus first chose the most improbable object to illustrate great power—a single mustard seed. It was likely the smallest article with which these first-century disciples were familiar.

> *"Small" is the consistent value of the Kingdom of God. God chooses the weakest, the youngest, the lowest, and the least in terms of pedigree, nationality, giftedness, education, or past reputation. ... Our smallness is actually the place where God demonstrates His grandeur and infinite might. The impossible task that awaits any*

> *church planter is not a task well suited for human strength. Human strength can build a fine religious organization but can never substitute for what can happen through a lowly mustard seed fully submitted to an omnipotent King.*[20]

Then in Luke 13, Jesus moves to the illustration of yeast. The action of the yeast (fermentation) is unseen, but its effect is pervasive, radically transforming everything with which it comes in contact. Jesus is teaching us to see the significance of the insignificant.

The kingdom of God is revealed, through both announcement and demonstration, when ordinary men and women live as citizens of the King in every neighborhood and public place that makes up a city. It is rarely dramatic or miraculous, but it is unstoppable.

ACTION

1. Keep a daily journal for at least one week. Note "God sightings and Spirit promptings" where God is urging you to participate in His kingdom agenda. After a few days, evaluate what you have written to see if any patterns have emerged. What have you seen afresh? How are you being encouraged to engage?

REFLECTION

1. Are you more church-centric or kingdom-centric? What about your church plant? How can you help establish a more kingdom-centric culture in your church plant?
2. How does the airport analogy make you think differently about the church?
3. How does Newbigin's language of sign, foretaste and instrument influence the way you think about the church and its relationship to the kingdom of God?
4. How might you help your church plant represent God's reign as a sign, foretaste and instrument of the kingdom?

CHAPTER SIX

JESUS SPIRITUALITY

Spirituality and mission belong inseparably together, like breathing in and breathing out.

– Barry Jones

Cross-shaped holiness is the kind of godliness that is distilled and intensified by engagement, suffering, service, and sacrifice.

– Michael Frost

Holiness is not gained by withdrawal from the world but by active, redemptive engagement in the world.

– Deb Hirsch

RETHINK

A major emphasis of the missional church conversation is the sent nature of our calling as the body of Christ—going into culture with the gospel, proclaiming and demonstrating the good news of the kingdom. In an earlier chapter, we discussed how the church is a sent, missionary people, which means we will most often need to *go* where people are. In the next major section of the book, we will talk about several specific missionary behaviors that are dependent upon our going into the places we live, work and play.

However, it is critical to not lose sight of the truth that we can- not go out under our own strength, understanding or power. To rely merely upon human reason or talent is to invite trouble along the way of mission. While we certainly want to encourage the church to engage in God's mission and make disciples as we "are going" (Matthew 28:19; Mark 16:15), we must not forget the "wait" commandment of Jesus (Luke 24:49). The power of the Holy Spirit is essential lest we go in our own strength and intellect.

Professor Paul Jensen writes on the sort of sickness that can develop when we establish a pace of life that is out of balance. When we overemphasize the *going* to the point that we lose the ability to hear from the Spirit, the effects can be destructive. Jensen argues that the elimination of time and space to hear from the Spirit leaves the church powerless:

> *The [elimination] of space and time ... can be viewed as a part of an addictive disease that has infected society and its institutions, including the church, much like a virus infects a computer hard drive. When the virus infects church and mission structures, its addictive pace leaves insufficient time and space for God in its operations, especially its leadership structures. Organizations with schedules crowded in God's name leave people empty. God's activity and fullness get frozen out. Though the machine continues its active pace, the organism of the Spirit becomes paralyzed...The organization becomes powerless over its addictive pace and needs God to free it from sick patterns. It needs treatment.*[21]

We do need treatment. We need the constant treatment of the Holy Spirit. As Jensen notes, too often our crowded schedules push away the Holy Spirit and drown out His voice. Our *going* must always be preceded by *waiting*—to be renewed and filled with the Spirit, not merely focused on strategy, techniques and creative ideas, as helpful as those are. *The Message* paraphrase provides a fitting rendering of Paul's words in 1 Corinthians:

> *I was unsure of how to go about this, and felt totally inadequate—I was scared to death, if you want the truth of it— and so nothing I said could have impressed you or anyone else. But the Message came through anyway. God's Spirit and God's power did it, which made it clear that your life of faith is a response to God's power, not to some fancy mental or emotional footwork by me or anyone else (1 Corinthians 2:3-5).*

SPIRITUALITY AND MISSION

We rarely pay much attention to the rhythm of our breathing unless something disrupts it. But the constant rhythm of breathing in and breathing out goes nonstop from the moment of our birth until the very last breath we take at death. The average adult takes between 12 and 18 breaths every minute, which means the rhythm of inhaling and exhaling occurs more than 20,000 times every single day. The rhythm of our breath is, in a sense, the rhythm of life.

In an excellent book titled *Dwell: Life with God for the World*, author Barry Jones speaks of this rhythm as a way to understand spirituality and mission:

> *There is a rhythm of life that pulses through the biblical vision of what it means to be human. A kind of breathing in and breathing out. An inhale and an exhale. The breathing in is our participation in the divine life. The breathing out, our participation in the divine mission. The breathing in is intimately connected to our experience of God's personal presence. It is life lived with God. The breathing out involves our participation in God's just reign. It is life lived for the sake of the world. The breathing in we often call "spirituality." And the breathing out we call "mission."*[22]

We don't read the Gospels for long without seeing Jesus leading His disciples into opportunities for the sake of inner formation. He would often invite them to join Him on getaways. At times, it was in one of their homes or on a mountaintop, an upper room, a garden, a boat, a shoreline or a walk through a wheat field. Jesus seemed to follow a self-imposed habit of discipline that frequently took Him away from the crowds and ministry into solitude, rest and prayer, both alone and in the small company of His twelve disciples.[23] These were times of breathing in.

These times of inhaling were almost always followed by periods of mission, or breathing out, that included preaching, healing, casting out demons and performing other miracles.

The point is that there is a critical and direct correlation between inward spirituality (time alone with the Father) and our mission. We will not fully understand *where* and *how* to engage as well as have the power to engage if we do not have significant time alone with the Father in listening prayer, reading of Scripture, worship, silence and participation in other classic spiritual disciplines. We simply *cannot* go under our own power!

Below is a brief, eye-opening sampling of the correlation between Jesus' frequent withdrawals from the masses and His empowered mission in both word and deed. His communion with the Father and the Spirit, whether alone or with others, fueled his ministry engagement.[24]

Withdrawal	*Empowerment*
Mark 1:11–13 Retreats to wilderness and is tempted. *Alone*	**Mark 1:13–34** Begins public ministry. Proclaims the gospel. Calls His disciples. Heals people and casts out demons.
Mark 1:35 Prays early in the morning. *Alone*	**Mark 1:36–3:16** Preaches in synagogues.

	Casts out demons. Heals people.
Mark 3:13–19 Goes up the mountain with the Twelve. *In Community*	**Mark 3:2–5:43** Teaches. Calms the storms. Casts out demons. Multiple healings.
Mark 6:30–37 Goes to solitary place for rest with the Twelve. *In Community*	**Mark 6:38–52** Walks on water. Calms storm. Feeds the 5000.
Mark 6:45–52 Prays in the night on the mountainside. *Alone*	**Mark 6:53–56** Many are healed by touching Him.
Mark 9:2 Retreats to mountaintop with three disciples. *In Community*	**Mark 9:2** Experiences transfiguration. Encounters Elijah and Moses.

Not only do we see this pattern of withdrawal and empowerment in the life of Jesus, but it is clear that the apostles and early Christians lived these same rhythms of inner formation. Frequency of prayer, fasting, shared meals and worship fueled their world-changing mission. Both Jesus and the apostles observed fixed hours of prayer, Sabbath keeping, getaways of solitude and the joy of the Jewish feasts and festivals. Unlike most of us today, they frequently broke away from the snare of productivity and busyness to be recharged and prepared for engagement. Here is a sampling from the book of Acts.[25]

COVOCATIONAL CHURCH PLANTING

Withdrawal	Empowerment
Acts 1:12–25 120 gather in the Upper Room. *In Community*	**Acts 1:26** Matthias appointed as one of the Twelve.
Acts 2:1 Believers wait on the Lord in solitude. *In Community*	**Acts 2:14–41** Peter proclaims, preaches. 3,000 souls added.
Acts 2:42 Believers in habit of prayer, fellowship, meal sharing, teaching. *In Community*	**Acts 2:43–47** Apostles perform signs, wonders. Believers share possessions. Salvations occur daily.
Acts 3:1 Peter and John participate in temple prayer hour. *In Community*	**Acts 3:2–4:4** Peter and John perform healing. Peter preaches, proclaims gospel. 5,000 new believers added.
Acts 4:23-30 Believers gather in prayer. *In Community*	**Acts 4:31–35** Believers filled with the Spirit. Word proclaimed with boldness. Believers experience unity. Possessions shared. No one needy. Atmosphere of grace develop
Acts 6:1–6 The Twelve and group of believers gather in prayer. *In Community*	**Acts 6:7** Proclamation of Word increases. Disciples multiply significantly. Priests converted.

Acts 9:8–12	Acts 9:10–18
Saul (Paul) waits and prays, fasting. *Alone*	Ananias experiences vision. Saul's eyes healed. Saul filled with the Spirit and baptized.
Acts 13:1–3	Acts 13:2–5
Antioch church leaders worship, fast, pray. *In Community*	Holy Spirit gives instructions. Barnabas and Saul sent in power of the Spirit. Gospel proclaimed in Jewish synagogues. Gospel proclaimed throughout region.

SPRITUALITY, HOLINESS, AND ENGAGEMENT

There is one other aspect of the breathing-in and breathing-out rhythms of spirituality and mission that should be addressed. Often when we think of the idea of spirituality, we equate it with the concept of holiness. Historically, spirituality was in the domain of a type of mysticism that sought God *apart* from a real engagement with the world. Many influential Christian spiritual writers developed their ideas and wrote their books on spirituality from monasteries or from churches that identified their main task as pastoral rather than missional or the making of disciples. Today, this has led to a view by many that can be defined as holiness by negation or holiness by avoidance. In other words, it is about a faith defined more by what we shouldn't do than by what we should. But that is simply not the way of Jesus. Christian spirituality in the way of Jesus ought to be a spirituality *with* and *for* the world.

Just think for a moment of the ministry of Jesus. He lived a type of holiness that caused "sinners" to flock to Him. People who were not like Jesus, liked Jesus. His brand of holiness didn't deter sinners from wanting to get up close and personal with Him. The Gospels are full of stories of sinners, the broken and the outcast trying to be near Him. Jesus was different. He wasn't like the other religious leaders of His day.

Think of the story of the woman with the issue of blood (Mark 5:25-30). She knew, as did everybody else, that her particular condition required a strict separation from the community and that "holy" ones should avoid all contact with people like her. And yet this holy man exuded something that caused her to reach out and touch him. She wasn't frightened or repelled by his form of holiness, for his holiness was inviting, alluring, enticing.[26]

Jesus's holiness was compelling. The Gospels give a crystal-clear picture of how the social castoffs longed to be around Jesus. Lepers, prostitutes, tax collectors, adulterers, Roman soldiers, Samaritans, Gentiles—the list goes on and on. Perhaps, even more amazing than sinners wanting to be around Jesus was that Jesus wanted to be around sinners. This, of course, was the whole purpose of Jesus' mission, to save "sinners" (Luke 19:10), and as a result, He practiced active proximity *with* them. Jesus, *the* Holy One, often went out of His way to connect with, or be seen with, those whom the other "holy ones" of the day never would have imagined being with. The holiness of Jesus is a redemptive, missional, people-embracing holiness that does not separate itself from the world, but rather liberates it.[27]

ACTION

1. At least four times this week, put aside 15 to 20 minutes to simply listen to the voice of the Lord. Don't talk, just listen. Don't *do*, just *be*. Open yourself to just hear His voice. Be sure to find a place where you can be alone with no distractions.
2. Take notes of what the Lord is sharing with you. Has He revealed anything to you about engagement? Are there aspects of brokenness in your context that you need to see? How might He be preparing you to engage that brokenness?

REFLECTION

1. Are you more of a *wait* or a *go* person? If you have a hard time waiting, do you see the importance of breathing in?
2. If you have a hard time waiting, what will you do to begin making time and space to breath in?
3. What strikes you about the rhythms of withdrawal and empowerment from the Gospel of Mark and the book of Acts? How does this change the way you view both aspects of this rhythm?
4. What thoughts do you have about the difference between a holiness by negation versus a holiness by engagement?

SECTION THREE

MISSIONAL ENGAGEMENT (MISSIOLOGY)

CHAPTER SEVEN

PLACE, PRAYER, AND THE PERSON OF PEACE

To the Jews I became as a Jew, in order to win Jews. To those under the law I became as one under the law (though not being myself under the law) that I might win those under the law. To those outside the law I became as one outside the law (not being outside the law of God but under the law of Christ) that I might win those outside the law. To the weak I became weak, that I might win the weak. I have become all things to all people, that by all means I might save some

– 1 Corinthians 9:20-22, ESV

Contextualization involves understanding a particular culture and adapting the communication of the gospel to the forms and expression of that culture so that obstacles to the gospel may be overcome.

RETHINK

As we move into a new section of the book the goal is to help you think missiologically. *Missiology* is a big word that simply means *the study of missions that seeks to identify the themes and motives in Scripture that compel God's people into engagement with the world.* These themes, among others, include the missio Dei (the mission of God), the Incarnation and the kingdom of God, topics that were addressed in chapters 2 and 3. However, it also describes the church's commitment to social justice, discipleship and evangelism. The bottom line is that missiology seeks to define the church's purposes in light of God's will for the world. That is really the overarching theme of this book—to rethink the purposes of your church plant in light of God's will to redeem and restore a broken world.

When considering missional engagement, we need to begin with the importance of understanding context or what some people refer to as *contextualization*. In the simplest terms, to contextualize means to put something into context.

In the above passage from 1 Corinthians, Paul suggests a missional posture upon himself toward different cultures and people. He does this to build relational bridges and have a better opportunity to clearly communicate the gospel. He is attempting to place the gospel into context in different settings. We might call this living a contextual life. Gleaning from Paul's words in this passage, we can develop a more comprehensive definition by stating that *contextualization involves understanding a particular culture and adapting the communication of the gospel to the forms and expression of that culture so that obstacles to the gospel may be overcome.*[28]

Historically, the practice of contextualization has largely been the work of cross-cultural missions. Missionaries sent to foreign lands had to spend significant time and effort to understand local cultures and discern how to best contextualize the gospel in particular settings. However, North American culture has experienced substantial change. Similar to the missionaries who were sent

PLACE: EXEGETING CONTEXT

Since everyone lives in a particular place (or context), the church's careful study of its context will help the church translate the truth of the gospel as good news for the culture to which it is sent. In the book *Kingdom First*, author Jeff Christopherson shares the importance of understanding a context,

> *The process of gaining an accurate understanding of context is critical for a planter to successfully be able to start a self-sustaining and reproducing new church. If the planter is indigenous to the specific place that he is planting, many findings from such a process will actually be intuitive knowledge. If the planter is indigenous to a nearby context but not the specific community in which he is considering planting, then working through a community exegesis process is helpful. If the planter is a cross-cultural church starter moving across significant geographical and cultural distance, then a contextual learning process is vital.*[29]

The contextual learning process mentioned in the above quote is sometimes referred to as *community exegesis*. Exegeting a community is the process of digging out and interpreting aspects within a context that are not readily observable on the surface. Through this process of exegeting a local community, a church planter can ensure a proper understanding of a particular context.

Church planting leader Barry Whitworth has developed a simple methodology to assist planters in accurately understanding the context of a potential planting location. Much of the following process has been adapted from Whitworth's work on contextualization.[30]

HOW TO EXEGETE A COMMUNITY

There are four primary areas of focus in the process of exegeting a community; they include gaining an accurate understanding of the *social, economic, physical* and *spiritual* climate of a particular context. By carefully examining and gaining a clear contextual picture of a community, a church planter can discover the need within a particular context, as well as methods and models that would likely be appropriate.

Under each of these four areas lies the same three-phase discovery process: (1) *Observation*: What am I seeing? Looking be- yond the superficial to understand how the community interacts. (2) *Conversation*: What am I hearing? Asking good questions followed by the discipline of unfiltered listening without prejudice or presumption. (3) *Implementation*: In light of what is learned, what probable steps should a church planter take?

Now let's examine the content of each of these four areas of community exegesis and suggest possible questions for each of the three points of discovery.

SOCIAL

The social structures of a community help to clarify how relationships are formed, as well as who is or is not connected in the com- munity. Greater understanding can be gained by asking:

Observation (What do I see?)
o What kind of interaction is happening between different generations?
o What is the diversity (socioeconomic, ethnic) of the community?
o What groups are connected or isolated?
o What groups appear to be slipping between the social cracks?
o How do people connect with one another, their community, their state or province?
o Are they open or resistant to interaction with outsiders?
o Who are the influential people or organizations in business?

Manufacturing? Schools? Government? Health care? Civic organizations?

Conversation (What do I hear?)
o Talk with the gatekeepers or power brokers in the community. Ask questions relating to the health of relationships in the community, as well as their perception of what is going well in the community and what could be improved upon. Ask specific questions on social problems and how effectively they are being addressed.
o Ask people questions about their community: Who lives in this community or neighborhood? Are there pockets of people of an ethnic background in your community? If so, where do they live?
o Listen carefully to what is being said to clerks, waiters and in general conversation in the community. Try to determine the lifestyles and worldviews with which people operate.
o What significant cultures and institutions are part of the fabric of their lives? Are you noticing any new construction in the community?
o How do people view "new things" beginning in their area?

Implementation (What should I do?)
o Once you have a better understanding of the community's attitudes toward the existing social structures, you are positioned to give early guidance for engagement.
o Begin to develop a plan of possible strategic relationships with the gatekeepers of the community.

ECONOMIC

Once you have gained an introductory understanding of the social climate of the community, you are ready to understand the financial environment that governs people's behavior. The economic structure of a community is significant because it can give people either a sense of stability or instability, growth or decline. Understanding the economy of the area can also help determine what the community generally values. People invest their time and money in what they deem to be important. Therefore, examining the economic implications of the context is far more involved than just demographic information on median incomes and education levels; it needs to get to values. Here are a few ways to discover the economic heartbeat of a community:

Observation (What do I see?)
o What evidence of struggle, despair, neglect and alienation do you see?
o What evidence of wealth and prosperity do you see?
o Is public transportation adequate?
o Is the community growing, stable, slowly declining or rapidly dying?
o Who determines public agendas—town council, churches, neighborhood associations?
o Does the community provide assistance for the needy?
o Are there service organizations for the children, elderly, singles?
o How well are homes in the community maintained?
o Are there "toys" in the driveway or yard (boats, RVs, pools, snowmobiles)?
o What are some noteworthy strengths or weaknesses in the following systems: public schools, housing, police services, health care, recreation?

Conversation (What do I hear?)
o Ask questions of community leaders and residents like: "If your community had extra money, how would you like to see it invested?" "If you had a week to put toward something you valued, what would that be?"
o What is the average commute to work for this community?
o Ask school personnel, "How actively do parents participate in the classroom?"
o When is the busiest time of day at the shopping center?
o Which day of the week is busiest?

COVOCATIONAL CHURCH PLANTING

Implementation (What should I do?)
o What activities do you enjoy that would also connect with this community?
o Ask: Because the people of the area value _____, a way to reach and build relationships would be to _____.

PHYSICAL

After you have scratched the surface of understanding the social and economic realities of our proposed context, it would be wise to next gain a deeper appreciation for the physical layout of the community. When trying to determine the location of where to start a new church, it becomes important to notice any geographic boundaries that may impede a new work. Also, what does the landscape tell you about the place and people?

Observation (What do I see?)
o What are some of the public places provided? Are they well kept?
o Are some paths of travel avoided by some residents?
o Does a railroad track, river or mountain divert people's travel or separate communities?
o Where are the schools located?
o How far do people travel to get to local healthcare?
o Where are local big-box stores located (Walmart, Lowes, Home Depot, etc.)?
o Are smaller stores located between housing and big-box areas?
o How close in proximity are local grocery stores?

Conversation (What do I hear?)
o Ride public transportation, if available, and ask people why they choose to use it.
o Ask recreational facilities about the distance their members travel in order to participate.
o Ask people if they know of a place to eat and see if they are familiar with the area.

o Another question may be, "Is there any place you would recommend I avoid while in your town? Why is that?"
o Ask, "What is the longest drive you would do weekly if it were something you wanted to attend?"
o Ask, "Is there a direction you don't want to drive to get somewhere? Why is that?"

Implementation (What should I do?)
o It is most likely that a single church plant will reach a maximum radius of or geographic area of _____.
o Make note of the boundary lines. (This could be geographic, transportation or other.) Likely, we will need to be planning other church plants in the area of _____ and _____ because _____.

SPIRITUAL

The fourth and final area of contextual investigation is that of the spiritual climate of the community. While all aspects of an exegetical process are designed to determine the activity of God, this one has a specific focus. You are studying the community to learn how people have been spiritually engaged in the past and how that is affecting the current reality.

Observation (What do I see?)
o Are the churches you have discovered growing, maintaining, or declining?
o How many churches are evangelistic in their purpose and plans?
o What are the "spiritual" places in the community besides churches (mosques, temples, Christian Science reading rooms, etc.)?
o Is the community giving to support charitable causes?
o Are there any Christian schools in the area?
o Are there any Christian nonprofit, parachurch or social agencies in the area?
o Are there any likely persons of peace in the community?

COVOCATIONAL CHURCH PLANTING

Conversation (What do I hear?)
o When visiting a Christian church, ask: "What significant spiritual markers in this community's history have affected the spiritual climate, either positively or negatively?" "What demographics have churches in this community found difficult to reach?" "What is their average age in attendance?" "What types of outreach methods to the unchurched are they currently employing?" "What is the most important lesson you have learned in serving your community?"
o Visit a local tattoo shop and ask them to tell you the most popular tattoo they do. Ask: "What themes seem to be the most popular to local customers?"
o Ask residents: "Where are the places of life, hope and beauty in the community?" "If you were able to make one spiritual request, what would it be?" "In what ways do you sense God's presence where you live?"

Implementation (What should I do?
o From the community exegesis exercise, I believe the spiritual climate for a new work is _____.
o There are deep spiritual wounds in this community from _____ and _____.
o Therefore, I would recommend that we concentrate on _____ and avoid _____.
o Persons of peace I discovered were_____.
o From my observations, the most underserved and spiritually hungry demographic in our community is _____.

Accurately understanding the context in which you will be planting will be one of the most important activities of the church planting process. You need to be extremely mindful to not "front-load" mission, where you have a preset strategy in mind for reaching your community. Instead, you must enter your context with a humble and teachable spirit, longing to discover the most effective ways to proclaim and demonstrate the gospel of the kingdom to your community.[31]

PRAYER

Another important aspect of contextualizing the gospel into a local community involves the power of prayer. Passages that help remind us of the importance of prayer regarding our contexts include Jeremiah 29 and Matthew 9. In Jeremiah, God instructs the prophet to "seek the welfare of the city where I have sent you into exile, and *pray* to the Lord on its behalf" (Jeremiah 29:7, ESV). We are to pray for the welfare—the shalom—of our cities. We are to pray that the city will thrive and prosper.

In Matthew 9, Jesus commands the disciples, "The harvest is plentiful, but the laborers are few; therefore, *pray* earnestly to the Lord of the harvest to send out laborers into his harvest" (Matthew 9:37-38, ESV). Jesus challenges us to pray for disciples to be sent into the harvest.

Praying for what God is doing in our cities is one crucial way to participate in the mission of God. As a church planter called to a particular place or people group, you need to be interceding on behalf of your city. Below is a list of prayers that serves as a guide for praying for your context. If needed, tweak the emphasis of each prayer. The idea is to have a specific focus each day to pray for your context.

Sunday—Pray that the gospel of the kingdom would be boldly proclaimed in every church in your city. Pray that people would gather to celebrate what God is doing in the lives of people throughout the city. Pray also that every church member would experience an increasing burden for the brokenness in the city and that they would desire to be equipped to be sent into that brokenness with the restorative message of Jesus.

Monday—Pray Isaiah 61:1-3 and Luke 4:18-19 for your city. Ask the Lord to help you see those who are the poor, the brokenhearted, the captives, the blind and the oppressed in your community and how to best engage them with the gospel.

Tuesday—Pray for your city to become a place of refuge for people seeking protection and justice. Pray for the quartet of the vulnerable, including the widow, the orphan, the foreigner and the poor. Pray Zechariah 7:9-10 over your city.

> *This is what the Lord Almighty said: "Administer true justice; show mercy and compassion to one another. Do not oppress the widow or the fatherless, the foreigner or the poor. Do not plot evil against each other" (Zechariah 7:9-10).*

Wednesday—Pray Matthew 6:10 over your city. Spend this day replacing the word *earth* with the name of your city or neighborhood.

Thursday—Pray for the people who influence your city.
- Pray for/with elected officials.
- Pray for/with social workers.
- Pray for/with educators.
- Pray for/with coaches.
- Pray for/with police officers and all neighborhoods to have protection and peace.
- Pray for/with firefighters for safety and security in the city.
- Pray for/with other pastors to have an impact on the city.

Friday—Pray for neighbors. Create a list of neighbors who live in the houses immediately in front, behind and next to your home. Whether you live in an apartment complex, a single-family home or a rural setting, make a list of neighbors. Pray that the Spirit would quicken their hearts and that He would create opportunities for you to begin to cultivate relationships.

Saturday—Pray that the Lord would show you persons of peace.

PERSON OF PEACE

One place we see the person-of-peace idea in action is in Luke 10:1-12, which is the story of Jesus sending out the 72. In His commissioning address to them, He instructs them to find a person of peace in each community:

> *When you enter a house, first say, "Peace to this house." If someone who promotes peace is there, your peace will rest on them; if not, it will return to you. Stay there, eating and drinking whatever*

> *they give you, for the worker deserves his wages. Do not move around from house to house (Luke 10:5- 7).*

Discussing how Jesus' person-of-peace strategy differs from the way we usually start churches, the authors of *The Shaping of Things to Come* write:

> *This was Jesus' church-planting strategy. He specifically in- structed them not to go door knocking from house to house. He advocated against taking a blanket approach to evangelism. Rather, his advance party was to visit various families until they had found a "man of peace." Then they were to concentrate their friendship on this one household.*
>
> *But few churches start this way. Many churches spend significant parts of their budget on advertising (print, electronic, letterbox), blanketing as many people as they can (in an attempt to get them to come to a church meeting). Finding a person of peace and basing our ministry there seems like a less effective method in the short term. But in the long term, a church-planting project that emerges out of the households of local, indigenous leaders will be much richer and more effective.*[32]

A person of peace is someone who has a web of relationships into which they invite us. As you take the missional-incarnational journey with your community, the person of peace will be a key person who will help you move forward. As you journey with the person of peace, consider how the Spirit is working in his or her life, but also in the lives of his or her extended relationships. In the New Testament, it wasn't unusual to see persons of peace and their entire households come to faith (Acts 16:31-34).[33]

ACTION

1. Work through each step of the "How to Exegete a Community" process, then find someone to share your discoveries.
2. Describe your prayer plan for praying for your specific context.

REFLECTION

1. Why is contextualization important to consider when planting a church?
2. What are two or three most significant discoveries in your exegeting the community exercise? What was surprising?
3. Explain the idea of a person of peace. How do you recognize a person of peace, and why does it matter? How can your community on the missional-incarnational journey join persons of peace in their web of relationships?

CHAPTER EIGHT

THE SPIRIT IN MISSION

While they were worshiping the Lord and fasting, the Holy Spirit said, "Set apart for me Barnabas and Saul for the work to which I have called them"

– Acts 13:2

For missionaries, the Spirit is an indispensable source of wisdom.

– Michael Frost

RETHINK

As stated in a previous chapter, the church is a missionary entity. The church doesn't just *send* missionaries; the church *is* the missionary. Individually and collectively as the body of Christ, we are a sent, missionary church. However, what we didn't consider until this chapter is the crucial aspect the Holy Spirit plays in this missionary agenda. Life with God and for the world must be lived in the presence and power of the Spirit, the third person of the triune God. But sadly, many Christians today are functional "Binitarians" rather than true Trinitarians in their understanding of and relation to God. God the Father we get (sort of). Jesus the Son we get (perhaps better). But the Holy Spirit? Many of us are not so sure.[34]

When it comes to the topic of mission, we need to recognize the Spirit as the director of the whole missionary enterprise. Let's consider three roles the Spirit plays in the missionary activity of the church:

THE SPIRIT TRANSFORMS US INTO THE IMAGE OF JESUS.

The apostle Paul wrote to the Christians in Galatia, "I am again in the pains of childbirth until Christ is formed in you" (Galatians 4:19). It is the work of the Spirit in us that makes us like Jesus. In 2 Corinthians, Paul writes,

> *And we all, who with unveiled faces contemplate the Lord's glory, are being transformed into his image with ever-in- creasing glory, which comes from the Lord, who is the Spirit (2 Corinthians 3:18, NIV).*

Discipleship (from spiritual awakening, to conversion, to maturity) is birthed in the Spirit, but it is also very much maintained in the Spirit. Discipleship involves growth into the "deep things of God" (1 Corinthians 2:10), and this simply cannot be achieved without the ongoing work of the Holy Spirit. It is the aim of every Christian to be transformed into the image of Jesus, and this, Paul says, is what the Spirit is up to in each of our lives.

As we discussed in the chapter on the spirituality of Jesus, it is important for us to understand that becoming like Jesus does not merely mean becoming holy in the narrow way in which that term is often understood. It isn't just about moral purity or being uncontaminated by the world. Instead, becoming like Jesus means learning increasingly to imitate His incarnate life (more on this in chapter 14). If we are to become like Jesus, we need a clear vision of what He was like. Jesus was the Incarnate One who dwelt among us to accomplish the mission of God. If we want to become like Him, then we too must learn what it means to live a missional life by the power of the Spirit in the places we live, work and play.

THE SPIRIT BEARS WITNESS TO THE GOSPEL OF JESUS.

Another sometimes overlooked aspect of the Holy Spirit's work is that conviction regarding the identity of Jesus is brought about by the Spirit's persuasive power. In the farewell discourse of John's Gospel, Jesus tells His followers that when the Spirit comes, "He will testify about me" (John 15:26). Elsewhere in the New Testament, the apostle Paul insists that "no one can say, 'Jesus is Lord,' except by the Holy Spirit" (1 Corinthians 12:3). These verses display the New Testament conviction that acceptance to the truth of Jesus and His good news comes as a result of the Spirit's work of bearing witness. As we will discuss more in future lessons, this reminds us that our job is to faithfully proclaim the story of Jesus and demonstrate His kingdom ethic, while letting the Spirit bring the conviction.

THE SPIRIT EMPOWERS US FOR THE MISSION OF JESUS.

> *After his suffering, he presented himself to them and gave many convincing proofs that he was alive. He appeared to them over a period of forty days and spoke about the kingdom of God. On one occasion, while he was eating with them, he gave them this command: "Do not leave Jerusalem, but wait for the gift my Father promised, which you have heard me speak about. For John baptized with water, but in a few days, you will be baptized with the Holy Spirit." Then they gathered around him and asked him, "Lord, are you at this time going to restore the kingdom to Israel?" He said to them: "It is not for you to know the times or dates the Father has set by his own authority. But you will receive power when the Holy Spirit comes on you; and you will be my witnesses in Jerusalem, and in all Judea and Samaria, and to the ends of the earth." (Acts 1:3-8, NIV)*

Jesus' words make clear that the task entrusted to His followers would require a power beyond themselves. They needed the power of the Spirit. It's important to note that when the Spirit's power is highlighted in the teaching of Jesus, it's not for the personal benefit of the "insiders." The power of the Spirit is not principally about the ecstatic spiritual experience of the Spirit-filled follower of Jesus but about the empowerment of that follower to participate in the mission of God.[35] N. T. Wright has said it well,

> Despite what you might think from some excitement in the previous generation about new spiritual experiences, God doesn't give people the Holy Spirit in order to let them enjoy the spiritual equivalent of a day at Disneyland. Of course, if you're downcast and gloomy, the fresh wind of God's Spirit can and often does give you a new perspective on everything, and above all grants a sense of God's presence, love, com- fort, and even joy. But the point of the Spirit is to enable those who follow Jesus to take into all the world the news that he is Lord, that he has won the victory over the forces of evil, that a new world has opened up, and that we are to help make it happen.[36]

In short, the Spirit has come to empower God's people to engage the mission of Jesus. We follow the Spirit in mission. Mission is a spiritual quest and is very close to the heart of God. To do it well, we must be willing to listen closely to the Spirit, discern His ways and align ourselves with His purposes.

PRACTICAL EFFECTS OF THE SPIRIT

To conclude this chapter, let's get a bit more practical by considering four missionary effects to discern if the Spirit is genuinely active in the church.

COVOCATIONAL CHURCH PLANTING

1. THERE WILL BE "JESUSY" PEOPLE.

As mentioned at the beginning of this chapter—but worth saying again—one of the works of the Spirit is to make us more like Jesus. Second Corinthians 3 is a passage dedicated to this concept. Paul ends with an insightful reflection on the inner spirituality of discipleship when he says, "And we all, who with unveiled faces reflect the Lord's glory, are being transformed into his [Jesus'] image with ever-increasing glory, which comes from the Lord, who is the Spirit" (v. 18).

When we grasp passages like this together with those who talk about the Spirit of Christ within us (for example, Romans 8), we can say that if we are not heading toward authentic Jesus-likeness and therefore engaged in discipleship, then there is something deeply wrong with our spirituality. If the Holy Spirit is genuinely at work, there will be a lot of "Jesusy" people hanging around— people who care for the things Jesus cares for and people with a heart for the lost, the vulnerable, the outcasts and the marginalized. Where the Spirit is, there will be Jesus-like disciples.

2. THERE WILL BE RISK AND ADVENTURE.

As discussed in Chapter 2, *missio Dei* is a term used to describe the mission of God. This *sentness (missio)* describes the nature of the Triune God Himself. God the Father *sends* the Son. God the Father and the Son *send* the Spirit (John 14:26; 15:26). And God the Father, the Son and the Spirit *send* the church. The Spirit is a missionary— so much so that when reading Acts, it's hard to tell whether the book should be titled the Acts of the Spirit or the Acts of the Apostles.[37] Like the apostles, we follow the Spirit in mission, which at times will involve risk and adventure. Unfortunately, too often the church in North America is risk adverse. We are afraid to step into the "risky" mission of Jesus because we fail to realize the Spirit is already at work in that place.

3. THERE WILL BE DISCOVERY AND DISCERNMENT.

Two major aspects of participating in God's mission involve discovering what He is doing in the contexts and people around us and discerning how He wants us to participate in His mission. The two "D" words of *discover* and *discern*, both involve the empowerment of the Spirit. To discover what God is doing, we have to become great listeners. Not only do we need to listen to the people around us, but we need to listen closely to the promptings of the Spirit regarding our contexts. What is the Spirit trying to show us? Where is the Spirit leading? But in addition to listening well to discover what God is doing, we need to listen, individually and collectively, to discern how God wants us to participate in what He is doing. Discovery and discernment are primarily activities of the Spirit.

4. THERE WILL BE LIBERATION AND TRANSFORMATION.

He unrolled the scroll and found the place where it was written, "The Spirit of the Lord is upon me, because he has anointed me to proclaim good news to the poor. He has sent me to proclaim liberty to the captives and recovering of sight to the blind, to set at liberty those who are oppressed, to proclaim the year of the Lord's favor" (Luke 4:17-19, ESV).

This passage in Luke 4 (see the larger context in Isaiah 61:1- 3) demonstrates that when the Holy Spirit is at work, there will be deep and profound liberation. The Spirit of the Lord anoints Jesus, and the result is liberation of people from all kinds of oppression. As the Risen Lord sent His Spirit to empower the church, we should expect no less in our experience of the Spirit. Paul is right in saying, "Now the Lord is the Spirit, and where the Spirit of the Lord is, there is freedom" (2 Corinthians 3:17). The presence of the Spirit frees people from all sorts of bondage: political, cultural, religious, ideological, psychological and demonic. "The Spirit brings freedom: He is the presence of the sovereign rule of God, a lordship that displaces all that cramps the human spirit as God intended it to be."[38]

ACTION

1. *Eliminate Distractions.* Find ways to avoid any distractions on the senses of touch, sight, smell, taste or sound. Music, noise in the distance, the tick of a clock, voices of people, the gentle breeze of the wind and even the written words of others in inspirational books—each can prove to be a distraction and prompt us to listen to what our ears or other senses are picking up. The quieter the room or surroundings, the more conducive it is to listening to the Holy Spirit.[39]
2. Spend at least one period of the week listening for the Spirit's voice. Keep a journal of Spirit nudges for at least one week. At the end of that time, evaluate what you have written to see if any patterns have emerged.

REFLECTION

1. Reflect on each of the three roles of the Spirit mentioned in this chapter. How do you see each of these roles reflected in your own life? What about the life of your church plant? What could you do to emphasize each of these roles in your church?
- *The Spirit Transforms Us into the Image of Jesus.*
- *The Spirit Bears Witness to the Gospel of Jesus.*
- *The Spirit Empowers Us for the Mission of Jesus.*
2. Reflect on the four practical aspects mentioned in this chapter. How do you see each of these aspects reflected in your own life? What about the life of your church plant? What could you do to emphasize each of these outcomes in your church?
- *There Will Be "Jesusy" People.*
- *There Will Be Risk and Adventure.*
- *There Will Be Discovery and Discernment.*
- *There Will Be Liberation and Transformation.*

3. What challenges do you face in setting aside time to listen for the Spirit's voice? What would help you protect that time as a regular habit?

CHAPTER NINE

ENGAGING 1ST PLACES

You'll be known as those who can fix anything, restore old ruins, rebuild and renovate, make the community livable again.

– Isaiah 58:12, The Message

God doesn't need our good works, but our neighbor does.

– Martin Luther

RETHINK

In the book *The Great Good Place*, sociologist Ray Oldenburg coins the language of first, second and third places. For Oldenburg, our first place is where we live, our second place is where we work (or the marketplace in general) and our third place is a setting of com- mon ground or "hangout." When referring to these different places, we can simply speak of them as the places we live, work and play. It is important to recognize that God has positioned us in each of these places for a missional purpose.

However, before examining each of these specific places from a missional engagement perspective, let's consider the importance of place in general. This is necessary because within many Christian circles we have accepted a distorted view of earthly place, which adversely affects the way we think about the places in which we live. There is a hymn from several decades ago titled *This World is Not My Home*. The popular refrain emphasizes that our time on this earth is only temporary.

> This world is not my home,
> I'm just a passing through.
> My treasures are laid up somewhere beyond the blue. The angels beckon me from heaven's open door,
> And I can't feel at home in this world anymore.[40]

This song illustrates a prevalent attitude held by Christians to-day: a belief that sees this world as little more than a holding station or terminal that provides temporary lodging as we await our final destination. In other words, this world is not our ultimate home. Moreover, the places we currently inhabit are fleeting and perishable. This widespread understanding of our existence on this earth holds that we are created for another world—another place.

This view of the world and our place in it is not entirely unexpected. The Bible does describe our standing in this world as that of aliens and sojourners in a foreign land. Furthermore, we know we are created as eternal beings. If we are followers of Jesus, we will spend eternity in heaven.

But what if, without losing any of the reality of our eternal existence, we began to appreciate the fact that this world *is* our home? What if we saw this place—our neighborhood, our city, our world—as a place of eternal significance? How might we care for our surroundings differently if we saw earthly places as part of the new creation? What if we stopped trying to escape this world and instead were reminded that God has given us care for all of creation, including the places we inhabit and those who inhabit them with us?

The Bible explains that the current creation is groaning as in labor, eagerly awaiting the day when it will give birth to the new (Romans 8:22). The resurrection of Jesus is a foreshadowing of future events. The corruptible will become incorruptible. The old will be transformed into the new. The new creation will not be totally new, but like the risen body of Jesus, it will be fashioned out of the old.[41]

However, instead of conceiving a re-creation of the world, many Christians view creation in a gnostic (or dualistic) kind of way. Heaven is our spiritual home and is good. The world is physical, corrupted by sin and, therefore, not good. And because the world is not good, it will one day be destroyed. This sacred-secular divide has done great harm to the way we think about and engage place. It keeps us shielded from the world God loves. Because of fear of the so-called secular, we fail to fully engage certain parts of the created world. By separating the sacred and secular, the physical and spiritual worlds, we have come to believe that driving across town to attend a church (sacred place) in another neighborhood can faithfully express our call to follow Jesus.[42] We don't even see how we have divorced our call to incarnational mission from God's activity in the ordinary or secular places of daily life.

Wendell Berry helps us rethink the sacred-secular divide when he declares, "There are no unsacred places; there are only sacred places and desecrated places."[43] If Berry is correct, then part of what it means to be a follower of Jesus is to "re-sacralize" the desecrated places. The apostle Paul says we are ambassadors of reconciliation (2 Corinthians 5:17-19). The ministry of reconciliation should certainly extend to—and perhaps even be rooted in—particular places.

Therefore, we must move beyond seeing this world as a meaningless, short-term dwelling as we await our final and more chief destination. Christianity is much more than that. And anyway, is that the kind of Christianity we really want? Is that the type of Christianity the world needs? What good are we to a world full of brokenness, alienation and hopelessness if followers of Jesus are simply waiting with our ticket punched for a trip to another world? If we are just passing through, why should we be concerned about this place?

COVOCATIONAL CHURCH PLANTING

This kind of attitude, even if not overtly exhibited, provides little motivation for getting our hands dirty in this life. There is no real need to interact with others—to learn who they are, their struggles and how we can be ministers of reconciliation. If we are simply sojourners from another land just passing through this one, it's too easy to neglect our immediate surroundings. That certainly wasn't how Jesus viewed this world. Even though He had a definite destination, and He knew where He was going, He didn't treat this world like He was merely passing through.

So now let's return to the discussion on the specific places where we live, work and play. When considering our "first place"—our home—there are at least two primary themes to examine: neighborliness (this chapter) and hospitality (chapter 12).

Most of us view our neighborhoods and cities as little more than where we live. We just hope for the best. We hope for a safe, peaceful, crime-free community with good schools, parks, employment opportunities, and arts and entertainment venues.

Philip Langdon, author of *A Better Place to Live*, laments this challenge as he reflects on his frequent bike rides through a neighborhood near his own suburban home:

> *I bike through a residential area that includes a large undeveloped property continually strewn with trash and broken trees. The people who live in the vicinity seem unable to get the owner or the town to clean it up—and seem incapable of organizing to clean it up themselves. When I bike past the area, it occurs to me that this is not a neighborhood; it is only a collection of unconnected individuals.*[44]

Langdon's last sentence is troubling. Sit down with just about any group and they will tell you they long to live in a neighborly neighborhood, but they don't know how to do it. Connecting naturally seems so—well, unnatural. The lack of a community experience perpetuates the middle-class psyche of individualism and privacy. And it grows in the petri dish of safety and security. In our heads, we have come to believe that independence is and should be normal. But, in our hearts, we know better. We long for connection with others. In our deepest parts, we are aware that normal life should be carried out interdependently.

For followers of Jesus, it is especially important that we lean into the community that is the living, breathing, tangible body of Christ and recognize the light it shines to a world wrapped in the throes of darkness. Every home on our street, every apartment in our building contains individuals and families that matter. The myriad concerns, fears, anxieties, hopes, dreams and longings that traffic in our own hearts are doing the same in every household around us. Who will be the ones to engage the disengaged—to connect the unconnected?[45]

LOVING STARTS WITH KNOWING

Take a look at the following image.

Jay Pathak and Dave Runyon, authors of *The Art of Neighboring*, use this exercise to help people gain a realistic picture of where they are as to knowing their neighborhood.[46] Start by picturing the grid as a plat of your own neighborhood. The middle box is your house or apartment, and the other eight boxes represent the residences closest to where you live. Concentrate on those eight boxes that represent the homes of others around you. Fill in the information for each of the bullet points in each box:

- Write the names of the people who live in each residence. You may only know first names. Write down what you know.
- Write down any relevant information about each person that you could only know by having spoken to the person.
- Write down something that's more in-depth. You would only know this information by having had deeper conversations. What are their goals in life? Is there a particular tragedy they have lived through? What do they believe about God, religion and so on?

Pathak and Runyon say that only about 10 percent of people can come up with the names of all eight of their neighbors, about 3 percent can provide information for the second bullet point, and less than 1 percent can fill the information for the last bullet point for each residence. Pathak jokingly says that the people in his church refer to this image as the "grid of shame." Now it isn't used to shame people, but it is an excellent illustration of the fact that most people do not know their neighbors by name. Obedience to Jesus' command to love our neighbor must start by knowing our neighbor by name.

SEEKING THE WELFARE OF MY CITY

When we make conscious and committed decisions—on a daily basis—to know our neighbors and seek the best for our neighborhoods and cities, life blossoms not only for us but also for those whose lives we touch. No matter how we reach out, even if it seems small to us, our cumulative actions become proportionately significant.

There is a fascinating passage in the Old Testament that provides a picture of what it looks like to live out incarnational presence. It actually gives practical instructions for digging into the places we live. It is especially helpful when Christians sense they are living in a world that is hostile toward their beliefs, or perhaps when we find ourselves living in a place that doesn't really feel like home.

In the prophetic book of Jeremiah, we read how the nation of Israel had forsaken God's Law and, as a result, found themselves taken into captivity and exiled far from their Jerusalem homeland. God had sent the Babylonian empire to discipline His people. As they were relocated to a foreign, idolatrous land, they began to hear that their time there would be short. False prophets were telling the nation of Israel that God would soon deliver them and that settling into this new, strange land was foolish. God's Word through the prophet Jeremiah to the exiles was quite different.

> *Thus says the Lord of hosts, the God of Israel, to all the exiles whom I have sent into exile from Jerusalem to Babylon: Build houses and live in them; plant gardens and eat their produce. Take wives and have sons and daughters; take wives for your sons, and give your daughters in marriage, that they may bear sons and daughters; multiply there, and do not decrease. But seek the welfare of the city where I have sent you into exile, and pray to the Lord on its behalf, for in its welfare you will find your welfare.*
>
> *– Jeremiah 29:4-7, ESV*

The words of Jeremiah were shocking. The premise of his message was that the exiles would be in Babylon for several generations—at least 70 years, a time period that included not only the reign of King Nebuchadnezzar but of his son and grandson (Jeremiah 25:11; 27:7; 29:10), and that the Israelites would simply need to come to terms with this fact. God was telling them to settle down and get used to being in this hostile, ungodly place.

It was toward this end that Jeremiah counseled his community not to be nostalgic for the past, for the past could not be recovered. Nor did he advise them to plan for insurrection, for there was no promise of their restoration in Jerusalem, at least not anytime soon. Nor yet was the community's survival tied to the remnant that remained in Jerusalem (Jeremiah 24:5-10). For Jeremiah, exile did not mean that God had abandoned Israel. Rather, exile was the place where God was at work. God's purposes with Israel, in other words, were served by the Babylonian invasion.

Jeremiah's instructions were more counterintuitive than they might at first seem. Jeremiah tells the Jews in exile to "seek the welfare" of their captors, to pray for the very people who destroyed their homeland because the welfare of the exiles and the captors were bound together. If God's purposes with Israel were really being fulfilled through their captivity, then as the exiles pursued the shalom of the home of their captors—Babylon—God would provide shalom for those in exile.[47]

What God instructs the exiles to do is actually rather ordinary. Consider the list from Jeremiah 29:

- Build houses and live in them
- Plant gardens and eat their produce
- Have children
- Marry off your children so they have children
- Seek the welfare of the city
- Pray for the welfare of the city

Nothing in this list is dramatic or miraculous. It is a list of normal, everyday activities. It could represent any person, regardless of income, social status, education, vocation or geographical location. The way the kingdom of God takes root in the lives of people and ultimately changes a city is by exiles living normal, everyday lives as citizens of the King in every neighborhood and public place that makes up a city. We build houses. We plant gardens. We have children. We seek the welfare of our city. Far more often than not, the ways of Jesus are indeed local and ordinary.[48]

WHERE TO START

Where do we start in the art of neighboring? The starting point lies in the word *ownership*. You must own the possibility in your neighborhood. Take ownership and act upon it. In the classic book *The Pursuit of God*, A. W. Tozer states:

> *Why do some persons "find" God in a way that others do not? Why does God manifest His presence to some and let others struggle along in the half-light of imperfect Christian experience? Of course, the will of God is the same for all. He has no favorites within His household. Pick at random a score of great saints whose lives and testimonies are widely known. Let them be Bible characters or well-known Chris- tians of post-biblical times. I venture to suggest that the one vital quality which they had in common was spiritual receptivity. Something in them was open to heaven, something urged them Godward. Without attempting anything like a profound analysis, I shall say simply that they had spiritual awareness and that they went on to cultivate it until it became the big- gest thing in their lives. They differed from the average person in that when they felt the inward longing they did something about it. They acquired the lifelong habit of spiritual response. They were not disobedient to the heavenly vision.[49]*

Praying over our neighbors by name and in light of any current crisis, concern or just normal life situation we are aware of keeps our neighbors' faces and lives on our hearts and constantly at the throne of God. Just imagine the power of prayer throughout a city when God's people pray for their neighbors on a consistent basis. Grab hold of Tozer's observation and "do something about it."

ACTION

1. As God's missionary people—the *sent* ones—it is incumbent upon us to constantly ask *missionary questions*. Some questions you should be asking regarding your neighborhood:
- How would a missionary live on my street?
- What would he or she notice is missing here?
- Who are the poor, marginalized and hurting in my neighborhood?
- What would *good news* be for my neighbors right here, right now?
- In what ways would my neighborhood be different if God's kingdom came here as it is in heaven?
2. Issue the challenge to your core group or leadership team to work through the neighborhood grid introduced in this chapter. Ask them to discuss ways to respond to the results of the neighborhood grid exercise.
3. Pray. Begin praying for your neighborhood each day. Pray for the neighbors you know by name as well as those you only know by description. Pray for those you have never met. Pray for your neighborhood as a whole that it becomes a place that experiences the peace and blessings of the Lord and the revelation of the gospel of the kingdom of heaven.

REFLECTION

1. How did the neighboring grid in this chapter challenge you? How many neighbors around your home do you know by name? What are your plans to get to know more neighbors?
2. How seriously have you considered your street and neighborhood to be your mission field?
3. In what ways can you and your church plant begin to seek the welfare of your city?

CHAPTER TEN

ENGAGING 2ND PLACES

Whatever you do, work heartily, as for the Lord and not for men, knowing that from the Lord you will receive the inheritance as your reward. You are serving the Lord Christ"

— Colossians 3:23–24, The Apostle Paul

If it falls to your lot to be a street sweeper, sweep the streets like Michelangelo painted pictures, like Shakespeare wrote poetry, like Beethoven composed music; sweep streets so well that all the host of heaven and earth will have to pause and say, "Here lived a great street sweeper, who swept his job well."

— Martin Luther King, Jr.

The priesthood of all believers did not make everyone into church workers; rather, it turned every kind of work into a sacred calling.

— Gene Edward Veith, Jr.

RETHINK

In the previous chapter, you were introduced to the language of first, second and third places. A first place is where we live, a second place is where we work, and a third place is a setting of common ground or "hangout." In this chapter, we will focus on second places, which are typically the settings in which we spend the second-greatest number of hours a day. Regarding living out of a missional posture, there are two key considerations to the concept of second places.

WORK MATTERS

First, it is important that Christians in the church have a proper understanding of the relationship between their faith and work. The language of "vocation" has become a helpful lens through which to view the Christian life and work in relation to God's activity in the world.

The idea of rethinking vocation must start with considering the sacred/secular divide, or what some people refer to as the problem of dualism. Dualism, simply put, is wrongly dividing something that should not be divided. The Greco-Roman idea was that the world is divided into two competing dominions: the sacred (spiritual) and the secular (material). Such a worldview tends to assume that the spiritual is the higher realm and the secular, or material world, is lacking deep meaning. Dualism leads to multiple divisions in thinking—including the division between the clergy (spiritual) and the laity (secular), the church (spiritual) and the world (secular), and between so-called religious practices (Bible study, prayer, worship) and supposed secular practices (work, art, eating).

This form of dualism happens most often in our understanding of vocation. The word *vocation* comes from the Latin *vocatio*, meaning a call, or summons. It is normally used to refer to a calling or occupation to which a person is drawn or for which a person is particularly suited. The problem of work dualism goes back to the fourth century when Augustine compartmentalized the way people lived when he spoke of the contemplative life and the active life. For

Augustine, the contemplative life was given to sacred things and deemed a higher calling, while the active life was given to secular things and regarded as a lower calling.

However, during the Protestant Reformation in the 1500s, Martin Luther rejected this division between sacred and secular vocations. He broadened the concept of vocation from a very narrow church focus (the priesthood, nuns or monks) to describe the life and work of *all* Christians in response to God's call. Luther argued that regardless of the vocation that God called someone to, it was sacred because it was God who did the calling. Therefore, it can be said that the doctrine of "the priesthood of all believers did not make everyone into church workers; rather, it turned every kind of work into a sacred calling."[50] Bottom line—all work matters!

But unfortunately, many Christians still see their work as nothing more than a necessary evil. They don't understand how their ordinary, everyday life is part of the mission of God. In the book *The Mission of God's People*, Christopher Wright speaks about how this distorted view of vocation sometimes makes it difficult for people to see that what they do outside the church is equally as important as what they might do inside the church.

> *God, it would seem, cares about the church and its affairs, about missions and missionaries, about getting people to heaven, but not about how society and its public places are conducted on earth. The result of such dichotomized thinking is an equally dichotomized Christian life. In fact, it is a dichotomy that gives many Christians a great deal of inner discomfort caused by the glaring disconnect between what they think God most wants and what they most have to do. Many of us invest most of the available time that matters (our working lives) in a place and a task that we have been led to believe does not really matter much to God—the so-called secular world of work—while struggling to find opportunities to give some leftover time to the only things we are told does matter to God—evangelism.*[51]

Therefore, part of helping people engage God's mission in the workplace must begin by giving them a fresh perspective on their vocation and helping them see how it fits into the broader picture of mission. We must help them understand that when they leave the house on Monday morning to "go to work," they do not some- how leave God behind.

WORK AS WORSHIP

Another reason all work matters is because of the connection Scripture makes between work and worship. The language of work in Genesis 2:15 ("*The Lord God took the man and put him in the garden of Eden to work it and keep it.*") is rooted in the Hebrew word *avodah*, which in English is translated *to cultivate*.

In the Old Testament, the word *avodah* is translated in several different ways. In some cases, it is rendered as *work, service* or *craftsmanship*. But other times, it is translated as *worship*. *Avodah* is used to describe the hard work of God's covenant people making bricks as slaves in Egypt (Exodus 1:14), the artists building the tabernacle (Exodus 35:24) and the fine craftsmanship of linen workers (1 Chronicles 4:21).

Avodah also appears in the context of Solomon dedicating the temple. Solomon employs this word as he instructs the priests and Levites regarding their service in leading corporate worship and praise of the one true God (2 Chronicles 8:14). Tom Nelson, in his book *Work Matters*, summarizes this important connection be- tween work and worship when he writes:

> *Whether it is making bricks, crafting fine linen or leading others in corporate praise and worship, the Old Testament writers present a seamless understanding of work and worship. Though there are distinct nuances to avodah, a common thread of meaning emerges where work, worship and service are inextricably linked and intricately connected. The various usages of this Hebrew word found first in Genesis 2:15 tell us that God's original design and desire is that our work and our*

> *worship would be a seamless way of living. Properly under- stood, our work is to be thoughtfully woven into the integral fabric of Christian vocation, for God designed and intended our work, our vocational calling, to be an act of God-honoring worship.[52]*

However, too often we think of worship as something we do on Sunday and work as something we do on Monday. This dichotomy is clearly not what God designed nor what He desires for our lives. God designed work to have both a vertical and horizontal dimension. We work to the glory of God (vertical) and for the furtherance of His mission and the common good (horizontal).

GOD IS AT WORK—AT OUR WORK

Building on the idea that all work is a sacred calling, the second key aspect of understanding second places is to realize that God is active in our workplaces. As Christians, we need to see that our work is not primarily about economic exchange. It is not about climbing the corporate ladder. It is not about achieving the American dream. Instead, it is about contributing *to* and participating *in* God's mission.

In a fascinating angle on vocation, Luther says that vocation is a mask of God. That is, God hides Himself in the workplace:

> *To speak of God being hidden is a way of describing His presence, as when a child hiding in the room is there, just not seen. To realize that the mundane activities that take up most of our lives—going to work, taking the kids to soccer practice, picking up a few things at the store, going to church—are hiding places for God can be revelation in itself. Most people seek God in mystical experiences, spectacular miracles and extraordinary acts they have to do. To find Him in vocation brings Him, literally, down to earth, makes us see how close He really is to us and transfigures everyday life.[53]*

In the simplest terms, Luther is reminding us that God is at work—at our work. God is active *in* and *through* our places of work; we just need to find Him there. As we discussed in chapter 2, we have to learn to *discover* where God is at work and then *discern* how He wants us to participate in what He is already doing. But as Luther suggests, sometimes what God is doing may not be obvious.

That is why the first step in discovering what God is doing is through listening. We must become *great* listeners. We look for God in the ordinary, in the sometimes commonplace, day-to-day activity of our work. We cultivate our ability to listen well to those in our workplace environment. As in any other missionary context, we need to pause and pay attention. Observe. Ask good questions. And listen to the fears, concerns, struggles and joys of those to whom God has sent us through our vocation. We must be constantly asking: What is God doing in *this* place, and what is God doing in the lives of those around me?

Once we discover what God is doing in our workplace, often the next step He is going to ask of us is to lean in relationally with coworkers. As we begin to *rethink* disciple-making, we will actually start to see our workplace as a place of discipleship.

Dallas Willard, who taught philosophy at the University of Southern California (USC), shares these words regarding the importance of the workplace and how it has been used by God to form him spiritually.

> *The place of discipleship is wherever I am now. It's whatever I am now, and whatever I am doing now. ... When I go to work at USC and I walk into class, that's my place of discipleship. That's the place where I am learning from Jesus how to do everything in the kingdom of God ... that's why it's important for me to understand that Jesus is, in fact, the smartest man in my field. He is the smartest man in your field. It doesn't matter what you're doing. If you are running a bank or a mercantile company or a manufacturing plant or a government office or whatever it is. He is the smartest man on the job.*[54]

Stop and think for a moment about your vocation. What is it that God has called you to do? Where is the place (or places) that you accomplish that calling? Do you see that place as a place of discipleship? When we begin to see your workplace as a primary place of discipleship, it will be life-changing. We will not simply "go to work." Instead, we will go to "do good work." We will go discovering what God is doing there. We will go to participate in God's mission of redemption. We will go to love and serve those to whom God has sent us. And we will go recognizing that our spiritual formation into Christlikeness is best seen not in what we do on Sunday, but how we work on Monday.[55]

ACTION

Pray these two prayers over the people in your missional community or core group and over the workplaces they represent. Provide these prayers for others to consistently pray over their own contexts.

Prayer for Vocations
God of heaven and earth, we pray for your kingdom to come, for your will to be done on earth as it is in heaven. Teach us to see our vocations and occupations as woven into your work in the world this week. For mothers at home who care for children, for those whose labor forms our common life in this city, the nation and the world, for those who serve the marketplace of ideas and commerce, for those whose creative gifts nourish us all, for those whose callings take them into the academy, for those who long for employment that satisfies their souls and serves you, for each one we pray, asking for your great mercy. Give us eyes to see that our work is holy to you, O Lord, even as our worship this day is holy to you. In the name of the Father, the Son and the Holy Spirit. Amen.

A Prayer for the Workplace
Heavenly Father, in your divine and gracious providence you have presently placed me in my workplace. It is my heart's desire that I

glorify you in and through my work today. May I do my work well, and may my mind be renewed as I meditate on the truths of your Word. Draw me near to you. Lord Jesus, let my workplace be a place of discipleship where I am learning from you as I work. As I walk in the power of the Holy Spirit, may the character qualities of Christlikeness increasingly be evident in my life. Lord, use my life and my work to further your redemptive purposes in the world and to enhance the common good. Amen.[56]

REFLECTION

1. How might you do your work as a God-honoring act of worship?
2. How would your coworkers describe you as a worker?
3. How does Jesus' work as a carpenter change the way you view your work?
4. Do you see your workplace as a place for discipleship? If not, why not? What would need to change for you to see your workplace in this way?
5. What does your local faith community celebrate? Do you celebrate vocation? How might you begin to incorporate vocational faithfulness into your community celebrations?

CHAPTER ELEVEN

ENGAGING 3RD PLACES

Great civilizations, like great cities, share a common feature. Evolving within them and crucial to their growth and refinement are distinctive informal public gathering places.

– Ray Oldenburg

Place gathers stories, relationships, memories.

– Eugene Peterson

RETHINK

It was in the book, *The Great Good Place* that author Ray Oldenburg introduced the language of first, second and third place. After discussing first and second places in the two previous chapters, it is time now to turn our attention to the concept of third places. A good place to start is with the subtitle of Oldenburg's book: *Cafes, Coffee Shops, Community Centers, Beauty Parlors, General Stores, Bars, Hangouts, and How They Get You Through the Day.* In the most basic sense, a third place is a public setting that hosts regular, voluntary and informal gatherings of people. It is a place to relax, a place people enjoy visiting. Third places provide the opportunity to know and be known.

But how are we to understand the distinctions of third places? How do you differentiate between these noteworthy hangouts and other gathering spots in a city? And what function do they play in the flourishing of a local community?

To begin, let's consider eight characteristics that Oldenburg identifies as being essential in the makeup of typical third places:

NEUTRAL GROUND

People are free to come and go as they please. No one person is required to play host. Everyone feels at home. There are no time requirements or invitations needed. Much of the time lived in first places (home) and second places (work) are structured, but not so in third places.

ACTS AS A LEVELER

A third place is an inclusive place. It is accessible to the general public. People from all walks of life gather. There are no social or eco- nomic status barriers. While there is a tendency for individuals to select their associates and friends from among those closest to them in social rank, third places serve to expand possibilities. Formal as- sociations tend to narrow and restrict them. Worldly status claims must be checked at the door of third places in order for everyone to be equals.

CONVERSATION IS THE MAIN ACTIVITY

Nothing more clearly indicates a third place than that the talk is lively, stimulating, colorful and engaging. Unlike corporate settings where status often dictates who may speak, when and for how long, third places provide the environment for every voice to be heard.

ACCESSIBLE AND ACCOMMODATING

The best third places are those to which one may go at almost any time of the day or evening with assurance that acquaintances will be there. They tend to be conveniently located, often within walking distance of a person's home.

THERE ARE REGULARS

What attracts regular visitors to a third place is not so much the establishment itself, but the fellow customers. The regulars give the third place its character and appeal. The regulars set the tone of hospitality. And while it is easy to recognize who the regulars are, unlike other places, newcomers are welcomed into the group.

LOW PROFILE

As a physical structure, third places are typically plain and unimpressive in appearance. They are not usually advertised. In most cases, they are located in older buildings, partly because newer places tend to emerge in prime retail locations that come with expectations of high-volume customer traffic. This runs contrary to the essential need to linger. It is in "hanging out" that people share conversation and life with one another.

MOOD IS PLAYFUL

With food, drink, games and conversation present, the mood is light and good-natured. Joy and acceptance overrule anxiety and alienation. The mood encourages people to stay longer and to come back repeatedly.

A HOME AWAY FROM HOME

At their core, third places are where people feel at home. They feel like they belong there and typically have a sense of ownership.[57]

Oldenburg argues that between the often private worlds of home and work, we all need a third place to informally gather with our neighbors. Whether that place is a coffee shop, a pub, a cafe, or a beauty salon or barbershop, the important thing is that it is open to everyone.

In the late 1980s and early 1990s, one of the more popular shows on American television provided perhaps the most iconic example of Oldenburg's definition of a third place. The television series was called *Cheers*, after the name of a sports bar in the heart of Boston.

One beloved scene took place in nearly every episode: When a particular regular would burst through the front door of the bar, everyone would shout his name in unison: "Norm!" The tagline for the show was "where everybody knows your name."

If you are familiar with the show, you can easily reflect on each of Oldenburg's characteristics and see how the sports bar served as the quintessential third place. There was nothing fancy about the setting. Everyone was welcome. There were obviously regulars. Conversations were always spirited. And a beautiful picture of how the bar acted as a leveler, regardless of status or vocation, was demonstrated every week as the psychiatrist shared a beer and banter with the mailman.

TYPICAL THIRD PLACES

Oldenburg's examples of third places include the local cafe, coffee shop, barbershop or beauty salon and neighborhood pub. It's interesting that the word *pub* originates from the phrase *public house*, which referred to a place that was open to the public, as opposed to a private dwelling. Like the local pub, these types of third places can be defined by each of the eight characteristics Oldenburg argues make up a genuine third place. That is why we call them typical.

ATYPICAL THIRD PLACES

However, there are many places that would not fit Oldenburg's definition of a third place, but they still provide opportunities for significant interactions. It is important to broaden our understanding of third places to consider these *atypical* places.

Atypical third places are many. They can include the library, gym, laundromat, farmer's market, community garden, park, grocery store, shopping mall, fitness center and any other place that you and others frequent regularly.

FIRST: IDENTIFY AND INCARNATE

Third places offer a unique opportunity for missions-minded people to do life in close proximity to others. But to connect with people in these places of common ground, we must first identify where they are in our community. Where do people gather to spend time with others? Where are the coffee houses, cafes, pubs and other hangouts? In some settings, these places will be obvious. However, in other neighborhoods you may need to work at identifying these gathering spots.

Once identified, we must seek ways to enter into (incarnate) these places. As discussed in chapter 3, incarnational presence involves rooting our lives into a local context. Over time we strive to move from being an occasional visitor to becoming one of the regulars. This issue of frequency is a main advantage of building relationships in third places. Your neighbor would probably not appreciate your knocking on his or her door every day to say hello and to cultivate a relationship. In fact, you would most likely be considered some type of stalker. But if you frequent a third place every day, you are referred to as a good customer.

Incarnating into a place, however, will involve more than simple frequency. We will also need to listen to discover where God is at work. When we listen, we heed the sounds, tune into them and consider them. The English word *listen* comes from two Anglo-Saxon words, one meaning *hearing* and the other meaning *to wait in suspense*.

At least some of our time spent in public places should be given toward hearing with an attitude of waiting in suspense. What is it we are going to hear from the Lord? What are we going to hear from those around us?

Any time you frequent a coffee shop, try to be sensitive to the surroundings. Simple things like getting to know the baristas, noting the regulars and listening to the conversations taking place are all important ways of pressing into the setting. It is really the art of noticing. We have to pause, minimize distractions and become mindful of what is happening around us.

You may need to stop thinking about your third place as your second office, but instead think of it more as your living room. Remember, third places are shared space. Even if you are working in your favorite third place, try to eliminate barriers that might keep people from approaching you and striking up a conversation. In other words, take out your ear buds. There is nothing that says "don't bother me" louder than someone with headphones.

SECOND: BE A PLACE MAKER

In addition to identifying third places that already exist in our communities, we will also need to create third-place environments where informal meeting places may not exist. We need to become place makers.

The language of place making originated in the 1960s, when activist Jane Jacobs, author of *The Death and Life of Great American Cities*, introduced pioneering ideas about designing cities for people, not just cars and shopping centers. Her work focused on the social and cultural importance of lively neighborhoods and inviting public places. While the concept of place making is much broader than our current discussion on third places, it does provide helpful language when considering taking ordinary space and turning it into meaningful place.

Being a place maker is simply about creating sweet spots in which people can connect. Place really does matter. If we long to see our communities once again thrive, we will need to recognize the importance of third places and discover how to both incarnate into those that already exist and learn to turn ordinary spaces into relationally vibrant places.[58]

ACTION

1. Consider the different types of third places in your community. Where are the typical third places? Make a list, including the name and location of each. Now do the same

with the atypical places. Think outside the box. In your community, where are the places you frequent that could serve as an atypical third place? Grocery store? Fitness center? Library? Farmer's market?
2. Write out what you will do to become more in tune with each of these places. How will you be more aware of your surroundings when you enter these third places? In what ways will you be more intentional to engage these places for the sake of the other?
3. Pray. Before entering each of the different types of third places mentioned in this lesson, pray that you would be more sensitive to what God is doing in that place. Ask the Spirit to give you not only insight into how He is at work in the lives of others, but the wisdom and courage to lean into what He is doing.

REFLECTION

1. Reflect on the quote from Oldenburg at the very beginning of this chapter: "Great civilizations, like great cities, share a common feature. Evolving within them and crucial to their growth and refinement are distinctive informal public gathering places."
2. Have you ever thought about the importance of informal public life? Do you have those places in your own life? Can you see the importance they can play in the lives of others?
3. How might you go about entering into some of the third places that you listed above?
4. How could you create a third-place environment in your neighborhood?

CHAPTER TWELVE

BIBLICAL HOSPITALITY

If there is any concept worth restoring to its original depth and evocative potential, it is the concept of hospitality.

— Henri Nouwen

When we fear the other, our own world gets smaller and smaller. It is only when we open our homes and our lives to the stranger that we can see our world begin to enlarge. The real question is not "How dangerous is that stranger?" The real question is, how dangerous will I become if I am not more open?

— Brad Brisco

RETHINK

What is the first thing that comes to mind when you hear the word *hospitality*? For most people, images emerge of entertaining around meals or inviting friends into our homes for a night of fun and games. Now let's be clear. There is nothing wrong with sharing a meal with friends and family. Genuine, biblical hospitality, however, is much more than entertaining.

One simple distinction between biblical hospitality and entertaining is that the latter puts the focus on the host. In doing so, it can actually become an issue of pride. As the host, we are concerned what others will think about our home. We wonder, how will our home reflect on us? There is a desire to impress our guests. We want them to like us and the place we live. We worry about making everything just right. If our home isn't perfectly clean and decorated, how can we possibly entertain guests? This sort of hospitality can easily become more about *appearances* than *persons*.

With biblical hospitality, the focus is not on us as hosts. In- stead, it is on our guests. Our concern is not on the appearance of our home, but on the needs and concerns of those invited into our homes. What do we have to learn from our guests? What do they have to share? What needs do our guests bring with them that we can address? What promise are they carrying with them that we need to receive? What about our guest can we celebrate during our time together? Soon, we discover that the distinction between host and guest proves to be artificial. Our differences evaporate into a mutual sense of being included.[59]

Scripture gives further clarity on the concept of hospitality, as well as its crucial importance. The Bible holds hospitality—especially toward strangers—in high regard. The laws prescribing holiness in the book of Leviticus include reference to hospitality:

> *When a foreigner resides among you in your land, do not mis- treat them. The foreigner residing among you must be treated as your native-born. Love them as yourself, for you were foreigners in Egypt. I am the Lord your God.*
>
> *– Leviticus 19:33-34, NIV*

We are not only to do no wrong to those outside our community; we are to actively love the "foreigner" as we love ourselves. In this passage, the better translation of "as yourself" (*kamocha*) is "for he is like you." We, too, were aliens once—outside the community—yet God treated us as native-born. The point is reiterated in

Deuteronomy 10:19: "…you are to love those who are foreigners, for you yourselves were foreigners in Egypt."

In the New Testament, this mandate is given with even more force as Jesus teaches in the parable of the sheep and the goats:

> *Then the King will say to those on his right, "Come, you who are blessed by my Father; take your inheritance, the kingdom prepared for you since the creation of the world. For I was hungry and you gave me something to eat, I was thirsty and you gave me something to drink, I was a stranger and you invited me in, I needed clothes and you clothed me, I was sick and you looked after me, I was in prison and you came to visit me."*
>
> *Then the righteous will answer him, "Lord, when did we see you hungry and feed you, or thirsty and give you something to drink? When did we see you a stranger and invite you in, or needing clothes and clothe you? When did we see you sick or in prison and go to visit you?"*
>
> *The King will reply, "Truly I tell you, whatever you did for one of the least of these brothers and sisters of mine, you did for me"*
>
> *— Matthew 25:34-40, NIV*

To welcome the stranger is to welcome Christ. "Believer or nonbeliever, attractive or unattractive, admirable or disreputable, upstanding or vile—the stranger is marked by the image of God."[60] Therefore, we are called to love.

The Greek word for *hospitality* in the New Testament makes this perfectly clear. It is the word *philoxenia*, which is a combination of two words: *love* (*phileo*) and the word for *stranger* (*xenos*). It literally means *love of stranger*.

Loving the stranger was a vital element in the life of the early church. Numerous passages speak to the importance of hospitality. Just a few include:

> *Rejoice in hope, be patient in suffering, persevere in prayer. Contribute to the needs of the saints; extend hospitality to strangers.*
>
> *— Romans 12:12-13, NRSV*

> *Do not forget to show hospitality to strangers, for by so doing some people have shown hospitality to angels without knowing it.*
>
> *— Hebrews 13:2, NIV*

> *The overseer is to be above reproach, faithful to his wife, temperate, self-controlled, respectable, hospitable, able to teach.*
>
> *— 1 Timothy 3:2, NIV*

> *Offer hospitality to one another without grumbling.*
>
> *—1 Peter 4:9*

Another aspect of hospitality is important to note. It is not just for the benefit of the other. There is also something extraordinary that is gained when we receive the stranger.

> *When you give a dinner or a banquet, do not invite your friends or your brothers or your relatives or rich neighbors, lest they also invite you in return and you be repaid. But when you give a feast, invite the poor, the crippled, the lame, the blind, and you will be blessed, because they cannot repay you.*
>
> *— Luke 14:12-14, ESV*

The practice of biblical hospitality is unique because it reaches out to those who cannot reciprocate. In most cases, when we invite friends into our homes for dinner, there is an expectation that they will return the favor and have us into their home. But the point of this passage is that customary "pay back" hospitality is of no great merit to God. The very best hospitality is that which is bestowed, not exchanged.[61]

The Jewish philosopher Emmanuel Levinas said the only thing that really converts people at a deep level is seeing "the face of the other." Welcoming and empathizing with the other leads to transformation of the whole person. This interchange is prepared to transform both persons—the seer and the seen.[62] In a sense, we need the stranger for our own conversion from our individualism, self-centeredness and our tendencies toward self-preservation and exclusion.

Being included is really at the core of biblical hospitality. If we had to take all this talk about loving strangers and welcoming people into our lives and homes and boil it all down into one word, it would be the word *inclusion*. As followers of Jesus, we are called to be radically inclusive people. We should be quick to include others into our lives.

The opposite of inclusion is exclusion, which always involves dismissal and rejection. Can you remember a time in your life when you were excluded? Stop and think for a moment. How did being excluded from the lives and activities of others make you feel? Being left out, rejected by others, is deeply hurtful. The sad reality is that thousands of people live daily lives of exclusion. They are not welcomed—by anyone. They are left to exist at the margins, on the fringes of society, living relationally impoverished lives. It is not right. No one is brought into this world to live a life of isolation. We do not flourish as human beings when we know no one and no one knows us; we do not flourish as human beings when we belong to no place, and no place cares about us. When we have no sense of relationship to people or place, we have no sense of responsibility to people or place. We are created as social, relational beings who are made for community. Hospitality, when rightly understood and pursued, has the power to break the bonds of isolation and exclusion.

Exclusion is not the way of Jesus. But if hospitality is clearly presented in Scripture, and if it gives us the capacity to overcome the relational separation that is so prevalent today, then why do we continue to exclude others? When did we lose the capacity to give and receive hospitality? Why has it virtually disappeared from the life of the church? The reasons are undoubtedly complex, but the two greatest enemies of hospitality appear to be *fear* and *lack of margin*. Let's conclude this chapter by considering how fear has become a barrier to being radically hospitable, and we will examine the topic of margin more completely in chapter 21.

XENOPHOBIA

In sharp contrast to the Greek word *philoxenia*, which means love of stranger, you may have heard the more popular word *xenophobia*, which is the fear or even hatred of the stranger or foreigner. While there is certainly a clinical expression of xenophobia, there is a level of fear of the stranger that has unfortunately been conditioned in us all over time.

The authors of *Radical Hospitality: Benedict's Way of Love* speak to the damaging effect fear has on our ability to welcome the stranger:

> *Fear is a thief. It will steal our peace of mind. But it also hijacks relationships, keeping us sealed up in our plastic world with a fragile sense of security. Being a people who fear the stranger, we have drained the life juices out of hospitality. The hospitality we explore here ... is not about sipping tea and making bland talk with people who live next door or work with you. Hospitality is a lively, courageous and convivial way of living that challenges our compulsion either to turn away or to turn inward and disconnect ourselves from others.*[63]

The average American, middle-class family has increasingly become a place to achieve safety and security from the "dangers" of secular society. The home has become a stronghold to protect the family from the evils of the world, rather than a place of welcome and hospitality. Writing on the typical American view of the home, Deb Hirsch provides this powerful critique:

> *This is "our" space, and those we may "invite" into that space are carefully chosen based on whether they will upset the delicate status quo, inconvenience us, or pose a threat to our perceived safety. In other words, visitors, especially strange ones, stress us out. And while this is in some sense culturally understandable, the negative result in terms of our spirituality is that the family has effectively become a pernicious idol. ... Culture has once again trumped our social responsibility. In such a situation, missional hospitality is seen as a threat, not as an opportunity to extend the kingdom; so an idol (a sphere of life dissociated from the claims of God) is born....*
>
> *Our families and our homes should be places where people can experience a foretaste of heaven, where the church is rightly viewed as a community of the redeemed from all walks of life. Instead, our fears restrict us from letting go of the control and safety we have spent years cultivating.*[64]

We wrongly assume that one of the greatest needs in our lives is safety. But what we need most is connection and acceptance from other human beings. Locks and fences can never do for our withered souls what genuine friendships can. Fear is indeed a thief. It will steal our ability to forge new relationships. Instead, we must see hospitality as an adventure that takes us to places we never dreamed of going.

ACTION

1. Identify the "strangers" in your neighborhood. Make a list of those who are in need of hospitality.
2. List three things that need to change to allow you to make hospitality a way of life. Develop a plan to take steps toward

being more hospitable toward strangers. Who is the first stranger you will welcome?

How might you respond to these same questions from the perspective of your church?
1. Who are the strangers who live around the place where your church gathers?
2. What needs to change in order to allow your church to be more hospitable?

Pray. Begin to pray that God would give you fresh eyes to see those who are unwanted, unloved and uncared for, that He would give you the courage to do whatever it takes to live out the essence of biblical hospitality and love the stranger.

OPTIONAL ACTIONS

PRACTICAL WAYS TO LIVE OUT HOSPITALITY[65]
1. Invite people into your home. Invite neighbors for a meal, or perhaps dessert. Some people can more easily invite others over on the spur of the moment, but most people need to plan and prepare ahead. If that is you, then set a regular time each week or month to invite others into your home.
2. Make a list of people in both your faith community and in your neighborhood, who would be encouraged by your offer of hospitality. For those in your church, invite them to join you for lunch after a gathering. For those who live near- by, invite them to join you for lunch or a cookout. Some- times being outside is less threatening.
- Identify single parents in your neighborhood who need weekend childcare. Care for someone who is recovering from surgery. Provide short-term or long-term foster care. Talk with local pregnancy crisis centers about the use of your home for single mothers.
- Be a "home away from home" for college students or those serving in the military living away from home.

- Hospitality isn't always about inviting people "in." Provide hospitality at a local nursing home.

REFLECTION

1. Where do you have space in your home and in your life, that could be opened to others? Do you have room in your heart to love and serve someone who is unwanted, unloved and uncared for? Do you have room in your home to welcome someone, even temporarily?
2. Who in your neighborhood, your place of work or in the places you hang out is living a relationally impoverished life? How can you turn a stranger into a friend this week?
3. Besides welcoming people into our homes, in what other settings might we be more hospitable?
4. Reflect on the quote at the beginning of this chapter from Brad Brisco. How do you sometimes fear the stranger? How does that fear affect your family? How does it affect your church?
5. What tensions do you have from the Deb Hirsch quote? Does it resonate with the way you live? What steps might you take to overcome the desire for safety and security? In what ways does this apply to your church?

CHAPTER THIRTEEN

MISSIONAL DISCIPLESHIP

He is the one we proclaim, admonishing and teaching every- one with all wisdom, so that we may present everyone fully mature in Christ.

– Colossians 1:28

Jesus' call to discipleship was an invitation to choose a direction—"follow me"—and not a command to adopt a doctrinal manifesto or align with a set of religious rites.

– Reggie McNeal

I believe that the key to the health, the maintenance, the ex- tension and the renewal of the Church is not more evangelism, but more discipleship.

– Alan Hirsch

RETHINK

Like many aspects of the Christian life—church, mission, evangelism and even the gospel—we have reduced the concept of discipleship. In most church settings, discipleship is seen as an activity for believers. Many people think of evangelism as something you do with lost people, while discipleship is for those who have already made a decision to follow Christ.

As a result, discipleship has largely been limited to issues relating to our own personal morality and worked out in the context of the four walls of the church. We certainly don't want to neglect issues of personal morality. To strive for holiness and maturity in our own lives is extremely important, but it is only half the picture. The other half is our God-given responsibility to the world around us. In reducing discipleship to being just about us, we have severely neglected our biblical mandate to go and "make disciples."[66] Therefore, we need to *rethink* discipleship and broaden our understanding of disciple making. A kingdom perspective begins with people wherever they are on the belief continuum, often even before they know who Jesus is.

REFRAMING DISCIPLESHIP AND EVANGELISM

Put aside your normal understandings of evangelism (remember paradigm shifts), and let's reexamine the relationship between evangelism and discipleship, using the Great Commission as our guide.

We would all agree that if you are a disciple, then you are called to be a disciple maker, which should mean we will disciple people anywhere and everywhere. Jesus clearly states that we are to make disciples "as we are going" (Matthew 28:19).

Discipleship isn't simply something we do with believers after conversion, but instead it is *all* about discipleship, both pre-conversion discipleship and, if God does His thing, post-conversion discipleship. We know conversion is the work of the Spirit; our part is to be disciple makers who devote significant time and commitment to apprentice whoever wants to go on the journey with us. In other words, anytime we point people to the person, work and ways of Jesus, they are being discipled, whether they know it or not.

Now evangelism undoubtedly still takes place, but it happens within the context of discipleship rather than the other way around. We need to put evangelism back where it really belongs, as part of the Great Commission given to the church to make disciples of the nations. We will examine the topic of evangelism more fully in the next chapter.

As we rethink discipleship in this way, consider how Jesus discipled His followers in the Gospels. Scholars continue to debate the question of when the disciples were actually "born again." Some say John 20:22, where Jesus breathes the Spirit on them, and others say it was actually at Pentecost (Acts 2). Regardless, no one would say it took place before that. So, even "the Twelve" (and "the Seventy") were all what you might consider "pre-conversion disciples."

Moreover, the standard practice in the church in its first three centuries was that people had to prove their faithfulness to Jesus in discipleship before they were allowed to become part of the church! This was the original purpose of the catechisms. In other words, discipleship started long before a person became a convert. In movements that change the world, discipleship is an ethos—a way of life—not just an optional extra for the more dedicated Christians.[67]

Reframing evangelism around discipleship in this manner also creates better space for long-term, authentic relationships with the various people in our lives. We ought to have multiple, different kinds of discipling relationships. We will have pre-conversion discipling relationships where we are pointing people toward Jesus by sharing, in both word and deed, why we orient our lives about the person of Jesus. At the same time, we should also have post-conversion relationships where we are doing life with other people, growing together toward maturity in Christ.

BOUNDED SET (FENCES) AND CENTERED SET (WELLS)

To give you another framework to think differently about discipleship, consider the idea called *social set theory*, which is simply a model for *how* and *why* people gather together. When discussing the difference between groups of people and how they organize, some use the language of "bounded set" and "centered set." Here is the basic difference:

The **bounded** set (or sometimes called "closed set") describes a relational system that has clearly defined boundaries but no complete agreement on a set of ideas in the center. It is, therefore, hard at the edges and soft at the center. The existence of the boundaries, however, makes it very clear who is "in" and who is "out."

The **centered** set, on the other hand, is open. In many ways, a centered set is the exact opposite of the bounded ones. They have very clear ideas and vision at the center but have no real boundaries that people have to cross in order to join. Centered-set organizations are hard at the center and soft at the edges. It is more of an open invitation to join on the basis of values.

Missiologist Paul Hiebert applied this way of thinking about how people gather as the church.

He argued that when we understand the church as a "bounded-set" organization, then we develop hard edges or boundaries. In the case of the church, that usually means we focus on external characteristics, such as belief in a defined doctrinal statement or adherence to certain moral behaviors, like language or a dress code, or both. Therefore, a person's *belief* and *behavior* determine if he or she gets to *belong*. Viewed in this way, it is easy to see that most established institutions, including denominational systems, are bounded sets.

Hiebert then discusses the concept of the church as a centered set. From this perspective, Christians primarily define themselves as followers of the biblical Christ with Him as the defining center of their lives. Hiebert notes that while there is still a clear separation between Christians and non-Christians, the emphasis, however, would be on encouraging people to follow Christ, rather than on excluding others for the sake of preserving the purity of the set.

A sort of bottom line would be that bounded-set groups organize around a shared set of beliefs and values that are used as a "boundary" to determine who is in and who is out of the group. A bounded-set perspective is in many ways about a *destination*. A centered-set view, on the other hand, is more about a *direction*. It is defined by relationship and direction relative to a center. Those moving toward the center are considered part of the set, whereas those who are moving away from the center are not.

WELLS AND FENCES

A more practical way to understand the bounded- versus centered-set discussion is with the metaphor of wells and fences. In the book *The Shaping of Things to Come*, the authors (both from Australia) discuss the idea of social set theory by illustrating it with a practice in farming.

> *In some farming communities, the farmers might build fences around their properties to keep their livestock in and the livestock of neighboring farms out. This is a bounded set. But in rural communities where farms or ranches cover an enormous geographic area, fencing the property is out of the question. In our home of Australia, ranches are so vast that fences are superfluous. Under these conditions a farmer has to sink a bore and create a well, a precious water supply in the Outback. It is assumed that livestock, though they will stray, will never roam too far from the well, lest they die. This is a centered set. As long as there is a supply of clean water, the livestock will remain close by.*
>
> *Churches that see themselves as a centered set recognize that the gospel is so precious, so refreshing that, like a well in the Australian Outback, lovers of Christ will not stray too far from it. It is then a truly Christ-centered model. Rather than seeing people as Christian or non-Christian, as in or out, we would see people by their degree of distance from the center, Christ.*[68]

A centered-set perspective aligns much better with the broader view of discipleship as discussed in this chapter. The center must be

Jesus Himself. When He is at the center, a church will be concerned with fostering increasing closeness to Jesus in the lives of all those involved. A centered-set church must have a very clear set of beliefs, rooted in Christ and His teaching. Our job is to point people to the center, both in our pre-conversion and post-conversion relationships.

And when one gets closer to the center, the more Christlike one's behavior should become. Therefore, core members of the church will exhibit the features of Christ's radical lifestyle (love, generosity, healing, hospitality, forgiveness, mercy, peace and more), and those who have just begun the journey toward Christ (and whose lives may not exhibit such traits) are still seen as "belonging." Belonging is a key value. The growth toward the center of the set is the same as the process of discipleship.[69]

INPUTS AND OUTPUTS (OR FAITHFULNESS AND FRUITFULNESS)

But practically speaking what does this journey toward the center look like? What kinds of activities are involved in becoming more and more like Jesus? One helpful way to think about the behaviors of discipleship is to consider *inputs* and *outputs*.

Inputs are those activities or habits that we adopt today when desiring a particular change in the future. For example, when we have a goal to lose weight, an input might be to count calories or to exercise on a daily basis. We exercise (input) so we can lose weight or feel better physically (output). We engage in certain input activities to see some kind of output in the future. The two are unmistakably linked. Input goals are the things that you can do *today* that will produce the results that you want *tomorrow* (output goals). In the book *No Silver Bullets*, author Daniel Im argues that most churches use output goals, such as attendance and giving, when measuring whether someone is a mature disciple. Because outputs are often difficult to measure (more on the topic of measuring in chapter 19) the church defaults to simply counting how often members attend programs of the church and how much money they give. However, counting attendance and giving is clearly not an adequate way of knowing if someone is becoming more like Jesus.

To make the point that the church needs to focus equally on input goals, Im presents the results of a major study conducted by Lifeway Research that examined the state of discipleship in the church today. The study included interviews with 28 discipleship experts, a survey of 1,000 Protestant pastors, as well as 4,000 lay people throughout North America.

One of the more interesting aspects revealed in the research was the existence of certain *behaviors* that consistently show up in the lives of maturing disciples. These habits included behaviors like consistent engagement with the Bible, serving others, sharing Christ, exercising faith, obeying God and building relationships. The research showed that when people regularly engaged in these activities, they eventually exhibited the attributes of a maturing disciple. In other words, *faithfulness* to these behaviors (inputs) leads to *fruitfulness* of becoming more like Jesus (output).

The results from the Lifeway study fit well with the Disciple-Making Environment image shared in the Introduction. When you consider certain disciple-making inputs for your church plant think about them in light of the Venn diagram. Ask what input goals should be a part of your church plant that would help people develop Kingdom Thinking? What inputs are related to Missional Engagement? What about Biblical Community?

The research is clear that at the very least our disciple-making inputs must include consistent reading of the Bible. Therefore, discover the best way for your church plant to engage in Scripture reading. Perhaps it involves individual Bible reading plans? Different types of group Bible studies? Reading of Scripture in all corporate gatherings? Or all of the above. The point is that you have to discern the best way to incorporate Bible reading (input) into your church plant.

However, in light of the research also ask what input goals can get people serving others? How can people in your church better exercise their faith by engaging in God's "risky" mission? How can they build deeper relationships, that include both pre-conversion and post-conversion relationships? How can they step out of their comfort zone and point a broken world toward the person, work and ways of Jesus? If we want people to exhibit the evidence of maturity in Christ (love, radical generosity, hospitality, forgiveness, mercy, peace and more) we must help them engage in consistent disciple-making behaviors.

Remember, input goals are the things you can do *today* that will produce the results you want *tomorrow*.

ACTION

1. Begin to disciple a not-yet-believer. Try the approach suggested in this chapter of simply begin to invest in the lives of your neighbors and/or workmate. Try to see them as disciples of Jesus who have not yet encountered Jesus, and see your task as discipling them to become more like Jesus.

REFLECTION

1. When you think of making a disciple, whom do you think of first? The pool of potential men and women in your church who already believe or someone outside the faith?
2. To what degree is your church plant based on a bounded or centered set? How would you open things up a little?
3. How does the use of "wells and fences" help in your understanding of social set theory?
4. How will you incorporate the idea of inputs and outputs in your church plant? How will you articulate this idea with others?

CHAPTER FOURTEEN

INCARNATIONAL EVANGELISM

Mission is more than and different from recruitment to our brand of religion; it is alerting people to the universal reign of God through Christ.

— David Bosch

When we understand what it is to be truly missional—incarnated deeply within a local host community—we will find that evangelism is best done slowly, deliberately, in the context of a loving community.

— Michael Frost

Despite what people think, within the Christian family and out- side it, the point of Christianity isn't "to go to heaven when you die."

—N.T. Wright

RETHINK

What is evangelism?

Now that we have dealt with rethinking discipleship, let's turn our attention to the related topic of evangelism. As stated in chapter 2, the *missio Dei* is far bigger than simply evangelism. Certainly, evangelism is one of the aspects of our engagement in the mission of God, but not the only one. As the above quote from David Bosch states, "Mission is more than and different from recruitment to our brand of religion; it is alerting people to the universal reign of God through Christ." We alert with words *and* deeds. We illustrate with both *proclamation* and *demonstration*. We must see evangelism in this broader context.

Having said that, we need to be careful not to assume that unexplained action (demonstration) is evangelistic. As it's used in the New Testament, the term *evangelism* describes a verbal announcement. It is a declarative activity. Words are required.

But part of the problem with evangelism is many Christians feel they need to get the whole gospel out in one brief conversation. One of the primary reasons for this is many Christians are only ever in a position to "evangelize" strangers because all their friends are Christians. When the only evangelism we do is with strangers on airplanes or at the bus stop, we feel an understandable pressure to get all the bases covered, because this might be the only opportunity we (or they) get. "Evangelizing friends and neighbors, gradually, relationally, over an extended time, means that the breadth and beauty of the gospel can be expressed slowly without the urgency of the one-off pitch."[70]

In the book *Road to Missional*, evangelism professor Michael Frost paints a picture of what genuine relational evangelism ought to look like,

> *When we understand what it is to be truly missional—incarnated deeply within a local host*

> *community—we will find that evangelism is best done slowly, deliberately, in the context of a loving community. It takes time and multiple engagements. It requires the unbeliever to observe our lifestyle, see our demonstrations of the reign of God, test our values, enjoy our hospitality. And it must occur as a communal activity, not only as a solo venture. Unbelievers must see the nature and quality of the embodied gospel in community. And all the while, conversations, questions, discussions, and even debates occur wherein we can verbally express our devotion to the reign of God through Christ. No more billboards. No more television commercials. No more unsolicited mail. If evangelism is like a meal, think of it as being prepared in a slow cooker and served over a long night around a large table. It can't be microwaved. It can't be takeout.*[71]

Seeing evangelism in this broader environment helps us to understand that the experience of conversion is not ultimately a matter of knowing certain truths *about* Jesus; instead, it is the fruit of an immediate encounter *with* Jesus. Therefore, evangelism, in large part, is about fostering and cultivating opportunities for a person to meet Jesus. It is not about persuading people to accept certain truths, but it is about meeting Jesus in person and in real time. In the end, evangelism is *all* about Jesus.

EVANGELIST OR EVANGELISTIC?

When considering the topic of evangelism, it is helpful to make a distinction between the "gift of evangelism" and being "evangelistic." Contrary to the false idea that every believer ought to be an evangelist, the apostle Paul seems to assume a twofold approach when it comes to the ministry of evangelism. First, he affirms the gifting of the evangelist (interestingly, not the gift of evangelism, but that the evangelist himself or herself is the gift, especially in the context of Ephesians 4). And second, he writes as though all believers are to be evangelistic in their general orientation.

Paul clearly places himself in the first category, seeing his ministry as an evangelist. But it doesn't appear that he believes all Christians bear the responsibility for this same kind of bold proclamation to which he has been called. Note his description of this twofold approach in his letter to the Colossians:

> *Devote yourselves to prayer, being watchful and thankful. And pray for us, too, that God may open a door for our message, so that we may proclaim the mystery of Christ, for which I am in chains. Pray that I may proclaim it clearly, as I should. ...*
>
> *Be wise in the way you act toward outsiders; make the most of every opportunity. Let your conversation be always full of grace, seasoned with salt, so that you may know how to answer everyone.*
>
> *– Colossians 4:2-6, NIV*

For evangelists, Paul asks for opportunities to share Christ and for the courage to proclaim the gospel clearly (vv. 3-4). But he doesn't suggest the Colossians need to pray this for themselves. Rather, Paul says they should pray for the evangelists (people like Paul) and for them to be wise in their conduct toward outsiders and to look for opportunities to answer outsiders' questions when they arise (vv. 2,5-6). "When it comes to the spoken aspect of their ministries, evangelists are to *proclaim*, and believers are to *give answers*."[72]

It seems as if Paul assumed that the number of gifted evangelists wouldn't be great, and he believed that the gifted evangelists could be local (like Timothy—see 2 Timothy 4:5) or trans-local (like himself). He also seems to assume that some gifted evangelists would occupy a leadership function in local churches (see Ephesians 4:11), building up the church to be increasingly evangelistic. So, while it is an essential gifting for all churches, it isn't a gifting given to every single believer. Rather, the "normal" believers' function was to pray and conduct themselves, in word and deed, in such a way as to *provoke* unbelievers to question why they lived the way they did and, therefore, enter into an evangelistic dialogue.[73] Peter is in agreement with Paul when he writes in a well-known passage in 1 Peter:

> *Always be prepared to give an answer to everyone who asks you to give the reason for the hope that you have. But do this with gentleness and respect, keeping a clear conscience, so that those who speak maliciously against your good behavior in Christ may be ashamed of their slander. (3:15-16, NIV)*

To summarize, the biblical model is for leaders to: (1) identify, equip and mobilize gifted evangelists, and (2) inspire all believers to live "questionable lives." If all believers are leading the kind of lives that arouse curiosity and questions from the people around them, then opportunities for sharing the story of Jesus will flourish and chances for the gifted evangelists to boldly proclaim are increased.

This two-fold approach was so effective it literally transformed the Roman Empire. With evangelists and apologists such as Peter and Paul proclaiming the Gospel and defending its integrity in an era of polytheism and pagan superstition, literally hundreds of thousands of ordinary believers were infiltrating every aspect of society and living the kind of questionable lives that evoked curiosity in the Christian message.

They devoted themselves to sacrificial acts of kindness. They loved their enemies and forgave their persecutors. They cared for the poor and fed the hungry. In the brutality of life under Roman rule, they were the most stunningly different people anyone had ever seen.[74]

INCARNATIONAL EVANGELISM FRAMEWORK

What does it look like to live a "questionable life"? A life that evokes curiosity. One that is countercultural to the way most people live. One helpful framework for rethinking evangelism comes from a book titled *Flesh: Bringing the Incarnational Down to Earth*.

There are five key words that form a relational progression to remind us of the proper model of Jesus when it came to sharing the good news in both word and deed. The five words are: incarnation, reputation, conversation, confrontation and transformation. Let's examine each of these words and consider how they link together in the broader process of evangelism.

INCARNATION

In chapter 2, we discussed rethinking mission from an incarnational perspective. I shared that the Incarnation was God's ultimate missional participation in creation (John 3:16-17). When God entered our world in and through the person of Jesus, He came to live among us (*eskenosen*—literally, "set up a tent"): "The Word became flesh and blood, and moved into the neighborhood" (John 1:14, The Message).

If God's central way of reaching His world was to incarnate Himself in Jesus, then our way of reaching the world should likewise be incarnational. Now, it is important to acknowledge that the Incarnation of Jesus was a special, unrepeatable event. Further, as we enter the world of others, we certainly cannot take on another's identity in the fully integrated way that Jesus did. But if we make the appropriate distinction between *the* Incarnation with a capital "I" and incarnational mission, then we can say that *the* Incarnation should inform our posture toward our context. There are two words, both starting with the letter *p*, that help to bring clarity to the concept of incarnational mission in context.

The first word is *proximity*. Incarnational mission must involve living in close proximity to others. We cannot love and serve from a distance those to whom God has sent us. Just as Jesus took on flesh and blood and moved into the neighborhood, we must do likewise. This may require moving geographically closer to those to whom God has sent us. At the very least, it will demand creating time and space to be directly and actively involved in the lives of the people we are seeking to reach.

The concept of *presence*, the second word, moves beyond mere proximity to identification and surrender. Jesus identified *with* and advocated *for* those to whom He was called. As the Philippians passage makes clear, He humbled himself. He literally *emptied Himself* for the sake of others. This realization suggests an incarnational approach that calls us to relational identification with our neighbors that will lead to tangible acts of love and sacrifice.

It is helpful to recognize that Jesus' words from John 20:21, "As the Father has sent me, I am sending you," are most often used to emphasize the sending of the disciples and subsequently the church. But we must not neglect the first half of the passage. Jesus says, "As the Father has sent me." The word translated *as* (or in some translations *just as*) means *like* or *in a similar manner*. In other words, we need to be sent *like* Jesus was sent. To whom and in what manner was Jesus sent? He was sent to the down and outers of society. He was *with* and *for* tax collectors, the oppressed, the poor and the diseased. Again, taking Jesus as our example, we are called to do likewise.

The Gospels tell us that Jesus was a friend of sinners. Hear that—a friend. The Bible is full of examples of people inviting Jesus to meet and spend time with their friends. There was a sense of whimsical holiness about Jesus that drew people to Him. Someone once said that people who were not like Jesus liked Jesus. As followers of Jesus, shouldn't that also be true of us? Do you see why, in most cases, evangelism needs to start by being informed by the Incarnation? We need to be in close proximity to people. We need to do life *with* people.

REPUTATION

One result of truly doing life in close proximity to people is developing a good reputation. Evangelistic mission is most effective when we are living generous, hospitable, Spirit-led, Christlike lives as missionaries to our own neighborhoods. This is, of course, also true in our workplaces, as well as any of the social spaces we inhabit. Really anywhere we are around people, we have an opportunity to display a new way to be human. We have opportunities to extend the love, grace, mercy, hospitality and generosity of Jesus.

However, this is not only true for us individually; it is also true corporately or as a missional community or church plant. Missiologist Lesslie Newbigin is known for saying that "the only hermeneutic of the gospel is a congregation of men and women who believe it and live by it."[75] In other words, as a faith community truly lives out the ways of King Jesus, people will take notice. They will begin to see firsthand that the way genuine Jesus followers live is beautiful, intriguing and life-giving.

But unfortunately, in most cases Christianity in North America doesn't always have the best reputation. People haven't had the opportunity to observe up close how a genuine Jesus follower lives. Instead, a person may have seen a poor example of a Christian on television, or perhaps they work with someone who professes to be a Christian but doesn't live out the ways of Jesus, so they have a negative view of Christianity.

Think about it this way. The Incarnation of Jesus is ultimately about *representing* and *revealing* the *real* God to people. So, for us to be positioned to represent the real Jesus to people and develop a good reputation, we need to be *with* people. We need to incarnate into the places God has sent us and show people with our lives what it really means to follow Jesus.

CONVERSATION

When we do life with people and actually develop a good reputation, we *will* have meaningful conversations. Others will seek the truth in our lives. Author Hugh Halter argues that Jesus had opportunities for conversations because of the way He treated people.

> *Jesus was God and thus the most holy, true and perfect bing. And He was the most nonjudgmental person you would have ever met. People should have been intimidated and afraid to even approach Him, yet they came toward Him. People wanted to hear what He had to say about their broken lives. And when He finally spoke, they listened and changed. Jesus showed*

> *that you don't need to condemn a person be- fore that person will change—and that's why He said He did not come into the world to condemn but to save (John 3:17). And He did exactly that. People around Him didn't feel condemned, and they responded to His truth. He was chock-full, buckets overflowing, oozing out both grace and truth at the same time.*[76]

And when we do have those conversations, we need to talk about the King and His kingdom. We need to share that while we live in a broken world, full of chaos and pain, there is good news. From the book *Kingdom First*,

> *Although brokenness abounds within individuals, institutions and structural systems, there is good news. Jesus, our triumphant King, wants things to be much different in our damaged world. He desires to bring the peace of His atonement and His eternal victory into all the manifestations of brokenness in our world (according to Colossians 1:19-20). While we now live in the tension that we will not wholly see the fullness of Christ's peace until the new heaven and the new earth, there is a promise of peace where sorrow currently abounds. This is the gospel of the kingdom...*
>
> *According to Jesus, who is the gospel, He Himself proclaimed the good news, liberated captives, healed the sick, freed the oppressed and brought the Lord's favor to the least. All of this was Jesus' activity on this earth and His fulfillment of Isaiah's prophesy. This work of our King is what brings the kingdom of God to the dark and broken realities of a desperate world. Peace where there was chaos. Healing where there was pain. Comfort where there was deep sorrow. Wholeness where there was systemic fragmentation.*[77]

Unfortunately, many Christians don't have the opportunity to share this broader story of Jesus simply because we don't have friends who are not Christians. Therefore, when offered the chance to share the gospel, we have to rely on a sort of artificial, very reduced summary of the work of Jesus. In other cases, we have to create ways to "turn" conversations in a spiritual direction, because we are not doing life with lost people. If we were, there would be frequent opportunities to talk about the King we follow and share the story of how He has changed our perspective, not only on death but on life in the here and now.

We need to be prepared to share in very natural, relational conversations what it means to follow King Jesus. To follow Him through His atoning work on the cross. To follow Him in a cruciform-shaped life of discipleship. And to follow Him into the good news that through Christ, the in-breaking kingdom of heaven is at hand.

CONFRONTATION

If we have done the work of incarnation, reputation and conversation, we will have the opportunity to share the good news about the kingdom and its King. And we need to be prepared for the gospel (with the work of the Spirit) to confront. It will confront a per- son's sin. It will confront a person's worldview. It will confront their attitudes and assumptions about themselves as well as others. The gospel of the kingdom is so countercultural to the ways of the world that it will confront a person's sensibilities on every level. In most cases, that will not happen overnight. But if we are in a genuine relationship with people, there will be opportunities to have ongoing honest conversations about the reign of God through Christ. Ultimately, the goal of confrontation is to help people take ownership of their sin and let God reign over every single aspect of their lives.

TRANSFORMATION

When the Spirit does His work, the ultimate outcome is transformation. Notice the word *transformation* is used, not *conversion*. Now conversion is a starting point, but transformation is the full heart of the incarnation. Jesus came to change *everything* in us. "Whoever says he abides in him ought to walk in the same way in which he walked" (1 John 2:6, ESV). The apostle Paul shared with the Galatians that he was in anguish until "Christ was formed" in them (Galatians 4:19). This is a call far beyond conversion. It is the call to transformation.

However, it is also important to recognize that God designed us to be transformed *primarily* in community. Although we are all individual people and can relate to God without anyone else, we are not designed to grow by ourselves. Real transformation is a communal activity.

TWO FINAL THOUGHTS

There are two additional topics to briefly consider before concluding this chapter. First, the entire incarnational evangelism frame- work must to be bathed in prayer. We need to be praying through each of the five phases mentioned above. Particularly we should be praying for deepening relationships with those who do not know Jesus. We must pray that God gives us opportunities to incarnate into our context, live questionable "Jesusy" lives in front of a dying world and have life-changing conversations.

Second, while the most effective form of evangelism takes place through genuine relationships, we should acknowledge that there are times when the Spirit prompts us to share with others when the time we have with them may be limited. In those cases, we need to be prepared to explain the gospel in a summarized version. A very good tool to do just that is called "3 Circles." For more information search "3 Circles" at the North American Mission Board website, namb.net.

ACTION

- Review the twofold approach suggested in this chapter: (1) identify, equip and mobilize gifted evangelists, and (2) inspire all believers to live "questionable lives." Create a plan of how you will go about doing both of these tasks in your church plant.

REFLECTION

1. How has this chapter challenged or confirmed your view of evangelism?
2. What are your thoughts on Frost's view of the twofold approach to evangelism in Colossians 4? Which of the two best describes how you are wired?
3. What is your overall assessment of the incarnational evangelism framework? Work through each of the five words and share how you can help those in your church plant cultivate a posture of each.

SECTION FOUR

BIBLICAL COMMUNITY (ECCLESIOLOGY)

CHAPTER FIFTEEN

MISSIONARY FLOW

> *If we fail at engaging well and living as Christ would live among our neighbors and friends, we fail as missionaries and the culture doesn't see the visible beauty of the sent church.*
>
> *– Hugh Halter*

> *Community is a sign that love is possible in a materialistic world where people so often either ignore or fight each other.*
>
> *– Jean Vanier*

> *People are often attracted to the Christian community before they are attracted to the Christian message.*
>
> *– Tim Chester*

RETHINK

With this chapter, we begin a new section in the book on *Biblical Community*. A crucial aspect of becoming more like Jesus and following Him into mission involves the concept of biblical community. The adjective *biblical* is used here to differentiate this form of community from what most people think of when they hear the word. In the English language, we tend to use the word to refer to people with common interests or a shared belief system. In Spanish, the word for community is *comunidad*, which speaks to the love or concern one person has for another.

In the New Testament, the Greek word for community is *koinonia*, which is often translated *fellowship* or *partnership*. Perhaps the most well-known example of biblical community in Scripture is found in Acts 2:

> *And they devoted themselves to the apostles' teaching and the fellowship, to the breaking of bread and the prayers. And awe came upon every soul, and many wonders and signs were being done through the apostles. And all who believed were together and had all things in common. And they were selling their possessions and belongings and distributing the proceeds to all, as any had need. And day by day, attending the temple together and breaking bread in their homes, they received their food with glad and generous hearts, praising God and having favor with all the people. And the Lord added to their number day by day those who were being saved.*
>
> – Acts 2:42-47, ESV

Notice this passage states that the people devoted themselves to *the* fellowship. It also says that they had *all* things in common, and they took care of *any* need that someone might have. Each of these phrases communicates to the unique community that was being formed. It was a community of people who were truly devoted to one another.

This is a great picture of what it looks like to live in genuine biblical community. This kind of community is not only a good thing; it is an absolute necessity. God has created us *in* and *for* community—relationships of love with God and one another. Nothing is more essential for human flourishing.

The corporate nature of Christianity is illustrated by a recurring, but often overlooked, word in the teaching of the apostle Paul: *allelon*—which means *one another* or *each other*. The point is that the Christian faith is not an individual matter; everything is to be done with and for one another.

Within the community of those who live "in Christ" by the power of the Holy Spirit, persons are to be "members one of another" (Romans 12:5), "build each other up" (1 Thessalonians 5:11), "love one another with mutual affection" (Romans 12:10), "able to instruct one another" (Romans 15:14), "become slaves to one another" (Galatians 5:13) and "live in harmony with one another" (Romans 12:16). The relational aspect of biblical community is where and how love, joy, peace, patience, kindness, goodness, faithfulness, gentleness and self-control are lived out as believers "bear one another's burdens."[78]

However, there is more to the story of community. While we are undoubtedly called to be devoted to one another in the family of God, as a community we are created for much more. We are a family, but we are to be a family on mission. A community of genuine love rooted in the redemptive kingdom of God can never be an in-house enterprise, for such love is infectious and overflowing. We must realize that we live in community with others for the sake of the other, or better yet, for the sake of God's mission. The biblical narrative is the story of God's mission to restore community, both with Him and with each other.

If we are not careful, community can become insular. It can become too much about those in the group rather than those outside. It, in turn, becomes more about safety and comfort than about being an agent of God's redemptive mission.

Notice in the Acts passage it says that the followers of Jesus had "favor with all the people." The people, who devoted themselves to each other, also lived lives of such great love and generosity toward the outsider that they gained good will or favor with those who were not part of the fellowship. And as a result, the text says that people were being saved and added to the community day-by-day.

Theologian Lesslie Newbigin said that a believing community is the only hermeneutic of the gospel. A hermeneutic is a method of interpretation. In other words, people can only fully understand what the gospel truly means when a community of believers actually lives out the message.

Newbigin also said that the church, or biblical community, was to be both a foretaste and instrument of the kingdom. We are a foretaste of the kingdom when the manner in which we live gives the watching world a picture of the kingdom to come.

We are an instrument of the kingdom as we participate in God's mission. As a community, we strive to discover what God is doing in the lives of people around us and then discern how He wants us to participant in His redemptive purposes. We must see the church as an instrument, created by God, to be sent into the world to participate in what He is already doing.

The bottom line is that we are created for community. We are designed to be in community with God and with each other. But we must also understand that community can never be fully realized apart from mission. As a biblical community, we are both a called *and* sent people of God.

MISSIONARY FLOW

While it is crucial to be joined together in genuine biblical community with other believers, the default posture of many Christians is to either start with community (church), or as mentioned above, to allow community to become inward focused and self-serving. This is, at least in part, why this book is structured in the order of *Kingdom Thinking*, *Missional Engagement* and then *Biblical Community*. My hope is that reframing the order in which we think of mission will allow us to rethink the church planting process.

In the North American, post-Christian context in which we now live, we can't plant churches by simply starting a Sunday morning worship gathering. There may have been a day when we could build a cool website, rent a meeting space, send out flyers, put up banners and "launch" a church by starting a Sunday service. But those days are gone, at least in most North American contexts.

What is the alternative? We must begin with missionary activity. Instead of starting with "church" and trying to get to discipleship and mission, we must start with discipleship and mission and work toward church. This is what is meant by the phrase *missionary flow*. It's a simple way to think differently about the flow or direction of starting a new church, especially in light of a bivo or covocation- al posture. We need a new framework, a new way to think about planting that doesn't begin with Sunday.

Take a moment and examine the Missionary Flow graphic below.[79]

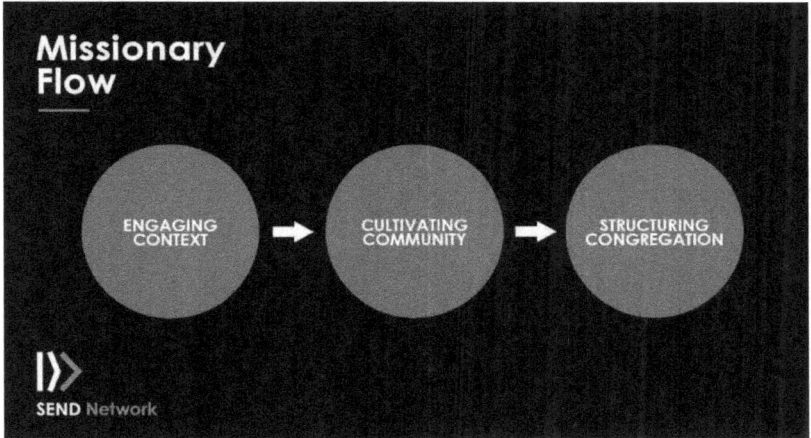

Notice the three circles, starting with "Engaging Context," which moves to "Cultivating Community," which then moves to "Structuring Congregation." Let's consider each of these three circles individually.

ENGAGING CONTEXT

This type of missionary flow begins from scratch. Too often church planters start with Christians from another church or they gather disconnected believers from around a city. This may be well-intentioned and *might* be better than nothing at all, but in most cases, that is simply starting a church with a church. That is not what we are talking about with missionary flow.

The first phase of any mission must involve contextualization. This begins with an understanding of the local setting, so you can best engage people relationally. As laid out in chapter 7, it involves place, prayer and persons of peace.

Along with understanding the context, we need to remember that we are a sent, missionary people. More specifically, it means we need to be reminded that we have *already* been sent. In other words, we have already been sent into our neighborhoods. We have already been sent to our workplaces. We have already been sent to the social spaces we inhabit each day. We don't have to wait, wondering where God might send us. Instead, we already live, work and play in these places for a purpose—the purpose of God's mission.

Once we recognize that we have been sent into the places we are already doing life, there are two over-arching missionary activities we need to live out. We need to *incarnate* and *participate*.

INCARNATE

We must allow the incarnation of Jesus to inform our posture toward our context. John 1:14 in *The Message* paraphrase reads: "The Word became flesh and blood, and moved into the neighborhood." As Jesus lives in us and through us, we *move in* to the neighborhoods and networks to which God has sent us. We put down roots. We stay. We incarnate into the local setting. Our contextual engagement must involve incarnating into local places.

PARTICIPATE

Once we incarnate into our context, we then begin the task of participating in what God is already doing. We participate in the *missio Dei*. Remember *missio Dei* means mission of God. The point is that it is *all* about God's mission. We, therefore, need to *discover* what God is already doing and then *discern* how He wants us to join Him. Participation in God's mission will involve becoming great observers and fantastic listeners. We listen to the Lord in prayer, and we listen to the community we are trying to reach. We need to be in tune to both.

The chapters in the previous section on *Missional Engagement* were all about engaging context. We examined multiple missionary behaviors including prayer, engaging neighborhoods, workplaces, third places, hospitality, missional discipleship, incarnational evangelism, etc. This is where your church planting efforts need to start. Identify the places and people to whom God has sent you. Incarnate into those places. Pray and listen for what God is doing. Discern how He wants you to participate as you begin to understand, relate to and connect with people. To repeat an earlier statement; instead of starting with church and trying to get to discipleship and mission, you must start with discipleship and mission and work toward church.

CULTIVATING COMMUNITY

The second circle in the image is titled *Cultivating Community*. The word *cultivating* speaks to the idea of nurturing. When we cultivate soil, we prepare it for planting. We have no power to actually make crops grow, but we can nurture certain conditions that will increase the likelihood for growth. Cultivating community is similar in many ways. We can't make community happen, but we can create opportunities and environments in which community can flourish.

We use the word *community* to make a distinction from the more customary word *church*. With the phrase *Cultivating Com- munity*, we want you to think about creating time and space for people to connect relationally with you, but also with each other. The key is that this space is not seen as church, but instead is a place where relationships are developed. The missionary phrase for this is *social momentum*.

Now examine the updated Missionary Flow graphic below. You will notice there are two additional phrases and arrows. Let's start with the idea of social momentum.

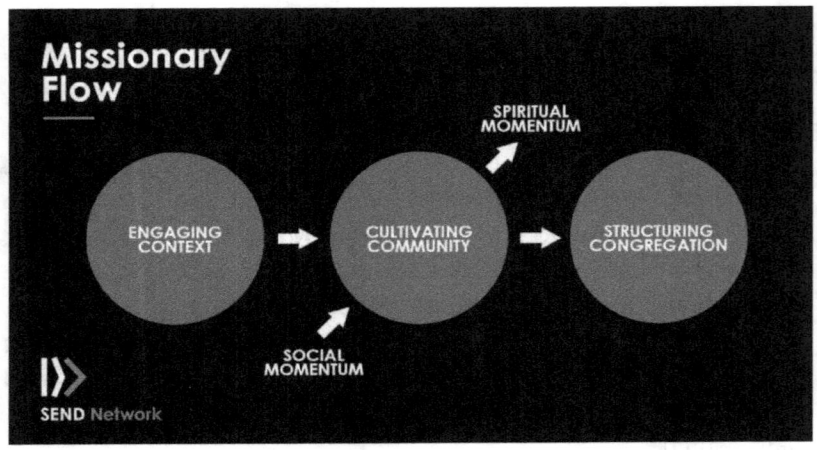

SOCIAL MOMENTUM

We have already stated the importance of starting with discipleship and mission when planting a new church in a missionary context. You need to begin by making individual, relational connections with people. The language of social momentum speaks to the need to create alternative spaces for Christians and non-Christians to connect, do life together and build relational equity (or momentum) before they ever consider attending a church program or activity.

The point being that unless you create a consistent, gathering environment—between engaging context and structuring congregation—that people can be invited to and be part of, you will never experience social momentum in your missionary engagement.

Here is another way to think about it. Most church planters are fairly good at engaging context. They work at getting to know their neighbors. They are intentional about making connections in coffee shops or at the gym. They pay careful attention at their workplaces for opportunities to make friends with coworkers. However, if there isn't an ongoing, somewhat informal, "get-together" for the planter to invite people to, then they will just have lots of good connections that never move beyond being acquaintances.

And for many church planters, after making those connections with new people, they don't have a clear vision of what to do next relationally. Too often, the only solution for a next step is to start the Sunday morning worship service so they have a church activity to which they can invite new people.

Now, there is certainly nothing wrong with inviting people to a church service, but in a missionary context, you need to consider an intermediate or in-between type of relational step. There needs to be some kind of regular, relational space to which you can easily and naturally invite people. Without such a consistent space to welcome the people you have met while engaging your context, you will *never* develop social momentum. Instead, you will simply have lots of relational connections that never move beyond knowing each other by name.

But what do those relational spaces look like? Find something you are already doing, or at least like to do, and develop a consistent rhythm whereby you can easily invite someone to join you. For example, maybe you do a fire pit in your backyard every Saturday night. Or perhaps it is the first Saturday night of every month. Maybe it is a game night you do once a week or once a month in your home. Sharing meals is always a great idea. You could schedule a neighborhood potluck once a month. The point is when you have that ongoing relational event that is consistently planned, it is natural to say to someone you connect with at work or in the neighborhood, "Hey, on the first Saturday night of every month we have a group of friends over to roast hot dogs and make s'mores around the fire pit. You know you would always be welcome to join us."

Creating time and space to develop social momentum will present many opportunities for pre-conversion discipleship and incarnational evangelism. But it will also provide a necessary opportunity for Christians and non-Christians to begin the process of cultivating community within a neighborhood or network. In the excellent book *Total Church*, the authors emphasize the importance of non-Christians having the opportunity to *belong* before making a commitment to *believe*.

> *People need to encounter the church as a network of relationships rather than a meeting you attend or a place you enter. Mission must involve not only contact between unbelievers and individual Christians, but between unbelievers and the Christian community. We want to build relationships with unbelievers. But we also need to introduce people to the net- work of relationships that make up that believing community so they can see Christian community in action. In our experience, people are often attracted to the Christian community before they are attracted to the Christian message. If a believing community is a persuasive apologetic for the gospel, then people need to be included to see that apologetic at work.*[80]

SPIRITUAL MOMENTUM

Now, back to the Missionary Flow image. The second phrase, with the arrow coming out of the Cultivating Community circle, are the words *Spiritual Momentum*. Similar to the previous idea of developing social momentum, you once again need to think about creating time and space, but in this case, it is to provide opportunities for people to grow spiritually.

It may be as simple as gathering to pray for one another. Or to read through the Gospels together. Or perhaps discuss what Scripture has to say to current events. The point is that if you are truly doing life with non-Christians and developing social momentum, there will be those who desire deeper, more meaningful conversations. Again, it should be natural and easy to say to someone that you "have a group of friends that meet once a week to pray for each other and talk about spiritual things."

If you are starting with, and connecting exclusively with non-Christians, this group that provides spiritual momentum may be something brand new. In other words, it may be formed directly out of the time and space you created to develop social momentum. However, if you have a group of Christians who are a part of your church planting team, this spiritual momentum group may actually be a missional community (discussed in the next chapter) to which you invite that person.

But regardless of the makeup of that group, the idea we want you to begin to process from this lesson is that we must create alternative times and spaces for genuine relationships to be cultivated. We live in a world where skepticism toward the church is rising. In some contexts, non-Christians are even hostile toward the church. In most cases, the only way to combat their negative attitudes to- ward the church is to show them firsthand what a grace-filled, loving, compassionate follower of Jesus looks like—and all the better if they can see and experience a community of "Jesusy" people. The bottom line is that we are creating space for people to experience genuine Christlike community. We want to give them the opportunity to *belong* before they may be ready to *believe*.

STRUCTURING CONGREGATION

Now let's move to the final circle in the Missionary Flow graphic, which is *Structuring a Congregation*. The point of the last circle is that if you are a church planter, there will come a time when you will begin to form or structure a congregation. There will be particular church issues you will need to consider. You will need to address topics of governance, meeting rhythms, administration, budgets, staffing, etc.

However, let me remind you once again, we are talking in this chapter about the importance of thinking like a missionary. Church planting is the outworking of mission and community. Or to restate that last sentence with the language of our Missionary Flow image: Structuring a congregation (church planting) is the outworking of engaging context (mission) and cultivating community. Church planting is the point where mission and community intersect. The church is God's mission strategy. At the heart of God's plan to bless the nations are the people of God. The church is formed *by* mission and is formed *for* mission.

ACTION

1. Engaging Context: Review the Missionary Flow graphic. List at least four engaging context missionary behaviors that will play a significant role in the life of your church plant. Which of these missionary practices will you model for the church?
2. Cultivating Community: Identify at least two ways you will create time and space to develop social momentum. In addition, articulate your plans for developing spiritual momentum.
3. Structuring Congregation: Make a list of the topics that you will eventually need to think about as you begin to structure or form a new church. List the names of those who can help you with each of those topics.

REFLECTION

1. How important do you think it is to rethink church planting? How is the missionary flow concept helpful for you to rethink planting?
2. What specifically does it look like for you to *incarnate* and *participate* in your context?
3. Engaging Context: Explain in your own words why it is important to start with engaging context. How do you under- stand the words *engaging* and *context*? How will you equip others to live out missionary behaviors? What do you think are the greatest barriers to engaging context? How will you address those barriers?
4. Cultivating Community: Explain the importance of cultivating community. Describe in your own words what is meant by *social momentum* and *spiritual momentum*. What do you think are the greatest barriers to cultivating community? How will you address those barriers?
5. Structuring Congregation: As you begin to form or structure the new church plant, how will you ensure that the

congregation doesn't lose the emphasis on engaging context and cultivating community?

CHAPTER SIXTEEN

STARTING MISSIONAL COMMUNITIES

To be the church is to be a learning community that seeks together in faith to know Jesus, to grow together in love for Jesus and to align our lives, mission and way of being in the world to the in-breaking of the reign of Christ.

– Gordon T. Smith

The purpose of missional communities is to be a source of radical hope, to witness to the new identity and vision, the new way of life that has become a social reality in Jesus Christ through the power of the Holy Spirit.

– Lois Barrett

Our ecclesiology should flow out of mission, not the other way around. Mission is the mother of adaptive ecclesiology; meaning if we start with engaging in God's mission there should be lots of wild and wonderful expressions of church.

The church does what it is and then organizes what it does.

– Brad Brisco

RETHINK

In the last chapter, the idea of missional communities as a place to foster spiritual momentum was introduced. Now let's consider key characteristics of missional communities as well as best practices on how to lead and multiply these communities.

WHY MISSIONAL COMMUNITIES?

The Christian life cannot be lived alone, nor can it be carried out as one person among thousands or even several dozen, which is often the context of American church gatherings. Instead, the best con- text for living as disciples of Jesus happens in community with a few other disciples, mutually committing to each other and to pursuing God's mission together.

When you look at the life and ministry of Jesus, you see Him discipling His followers as they experienced life together in com- munity. Jesus' way of discipleship cannot happen in one-on-one meetings alone. The church is the *body* of Christ, which has many parts. And it takes the body, committed to one another, to become more like Jesus. God intends for all of us to actively engage in disciple-making in light of our unique design and giftedness.
Church leader Jeff Vanderstelt articulates Jesus' disciple-making process this way,

> *Jesus didn't say, "Show up to class and I will train you." Nor did he say, "Attend synagogue and that will be sufficient." No, he called the disciples to join him on the mission ("Follow me"), and while they were on the mission with him, he trained them to be disciple-makers ("I will make you fishers of men"). In other words, Jesus taught them the basics of making disciples while they were on the mission of making disciples. They*

> *could observe everything Jesus said and did. ... They listened, watched, and learned in the everyday stuff of life. After a while, he invited them to share in some of the work he was doing. Sure, they messed up, a lot, but he was there to help, to correct, to clean up—to train them—while they were on his mission. They were in a disciple-making residency with Jesus.*[81]

In the midst of doing life in community, Jesus' followers learned what it meant to love God, love each other and engage in God's mission. It is within the environment of a missional community that these three gospel rhythms best thrive.

Missional communities (or what some call incarnational communities) are not smaller church services, Bible studies, small groups or some other program of the church. Instead, missional communities *are* the church. Many have been so conditioned by what they have experienced through typical church activities, such as weekend worship services or Sunday school, that they naturally seek to make missional communities fit what they have known before. But resist that temptation. Other programs and activities of the church are great for the purposes they serve, but they do not generally deliver on the purposes of missional communities.

WHAT IS A MISSIONAL COMMUNITY?

Definition: A missional community is a committed group of Jesus followers, the size of an extended family (12–25), empowered by the Spirit to participate in God's mission of redemption in a particular neighborhood and/or network.

There are seven key phrases in this definition that we want to describe further.

- *Committed group.* They are devoted to each other and to the mission of the community.
- *Jesus followers.* They are maturing disciples who are following Jesus' lead.
- *Extended family.* The group is small enough to care, yet large enough to dare.

- *Empowered by the Spirit.* They are formed and sent by the Spirit.
- *Participate in God's mission.* The *missio Dei* is the organizing principle of all they do.
- *Of redemption.* They will engage in both gospel proclamation and demonstration.
- *Neighborhood or network.* They are embedded in a neighborhood or network of relationships as an incarnational expression of the church.

Hopefully, this definition offers a framework to differentiate a missional community from a traditional small group, but at the same time it provides enough flexibility not to be too rigid. It is important as you define what a missional community looks like in your context that you not be too prescriptive. In other words, allow each missional community to be unique to its context and mission. All missional communities will not (and should not) look alike. Mission is the mother of adaptive ecclesiology, which means that if we begin with God's mission (missiology), there will be lots of wild and wonderful expressions of church (ecclesiology).

MISSIONAL COMMUNITY PRACTICES

While you want to be careful not to be too prescriptive on what a community looks like, there are intentional rhythms or practices that help to form healthy missional communities. Three significant patterns modeled on the life of Jesus provide a framework for the different aspects of a missional community life. While different words can be used to articulate each of the three patterns, they all refer to the dimensions of the "UPward" life with the Father, the "INward" dimension of life with the body of Christ and the "OUTward" dimension of engaging in God's mission. Let's examine each of these more fully.

UP (COMMUNION: TIME FOCUSED ON FATHER, SON, AND SPIRIT)

It is important to develop opportunities where a missional community puts itself in places where it can hear God speak. The "UP" component should involve prayer, hearing God's voice, worship and reading Scripture.

When we examine the life of Jesus, we see Him spending time with the Father. Many times, we read about Jesus praying. He spoke with the Father. He listened to the Father. He engaged regularly in worship and praise, personally and in gatherings at the synagogue and temple. But it is important to recognize that this communion aspect of community life is not merely a meeting. It's learning to live in the life of God throughout our ordinary life. Gathering to commune with and worship God certainly helps us live in God throughout the day and week, but communion and worship go beyond a mere meeting. It's a way of life; a rhythm of life.[82] Growing a Missional Community's UP

- Commit to a common Bible reading plan.
- Commit to a common prayer rhythm.
- Post the prayer needs of the community on a private Facebook page.
- Commit to praying the Psalms together on a daily basis.
- Host a night of worship and prayer with the focus being caring for one another.
- Attend a conference or seminar together that addresses your relationship with God.
- Identify three things in your community that seem impossible to change for the better and commit as a missional community to pray for them until something begins to move.
- Invite everyone to read a book on prayer, engaging the Holy Spirit or another topic in their spare time. Host a gathering to discuss what you're learning.

IN (COMMUNITY: TIME FOCUSED ON THOSE INSIDE THE BODY)

Jesus spent very intentional time with a small group. He invested in a limited number of people in order that they would have a greater impact and, at the same time, showed them a model for impacting the world. They literally did life together.

We then see that the early church had everything in common—the Greek word *koinonia* refers to a common life together. Those who had much shared with those who didn't have enough. They prayed together, broke bread together and labored together. They were not simply *like* family; they *were* family.

Growing a Missional Community's IN:
- Have consistent times for sharing meals together.
- Take up offerings for those who have financial needs.
- Take a camping trip together.
- Go to a family movie with all the kids!
- Go on a spiritual retreat for a day or two.
- Create opportunities for people to try new hobbies with other members of the community.
- Discover ways for your missional community to serve another community.
- Send the women or men on special gender-inclusive trips together.
- Have a date night where the teenagers watch the kids while couples go out for dinner and a movie together.

OUT (CO-MISSION: TIME FOCUSED ON THOSE OUTSIDE THE BODY)

Jesus met the needs He saw in the world around Him with God's love, grace and power. But He didn't do this alone. He most of-ten took His disciples with Him on mission. He proclaimed good news to the poor, released the captives, healed the sick, touched the lepers, fed the hungry and opened blind eyes (Isaiah 61:1-3; Luke 4). He proclaimed and demonstrated the gospel of the kingdom. In the book of Acts, we see the followers of Jesus doing the very same things they observed Jesus doing.

The "OUT" component (or co-mission) focuses on the fact that a missional community is the body of Christ. The community has been gifted and empowered by the Spirit to fully engage God's mission. A missional community is to be the hands and feet of Jesus in the local neighborhood or network where God has sent them to be peacemakers, reconcilers, activists, stewards of creation and announcers of the rule and reign of God through Christ. While there will be times God calls you to engage in His mission individually, the reality is that mission is best done as a community. Bottom line is that a missional community is a community on mission.

Growing a Missional Community's OUT:
- Conduct regular prayer-walks. Prayer-walks are also great ways to include kids.
- Host neighborhood/network cookouts, picnics, outdoor games, sports parties and movie nights.
- Reach out to those who share a common hobby.
- Participate in local city activities—parades, festivals, etc.
- Review chapters 7–14 for practical missionary behaviors.

ACTION

1. Revisit the definition for a missional community from this chapter. Attempt to memorize the language.
2. Discuss with your core team and/or missional community the definition.

REFLECTION

1. What are the differences between a traditional small group and a missional community? What would you say is the organizing principle of each?
2. Communion: What practice do you need to engage in that will help you draw nearer to God? What practice needs to

be incorporated into the life of your missional community to do the same?
3. Community: What practice do you need to engage in that will help you draw closer as a community? What practice needs to be incorporated into the life of your missional community to do the same?
4. Co-mission: What practice do you need to engage in that will help you better engage God's mission? What practice needs to be incorporated into the life of your missional community to do the same?

CHAPTER SEVENTEEN

APEST: ACTIVATING ALL THE PEOPLE OF GOD

In the biblical sense all Christians are priests and clergy, and this is a crucial starting point if we are to re-discover the true concept of ministry and leadership within the church.

– David Watson

In the New Testament there are functional distinctions be- tween various kinds of ministries but no hierarchical division between clergy and laity.

– Howard Snyder

RETHINK

In the very first chapter, I introduced an adage that speaks to the importance of considering change in an organization. The saying goes like this: "We are perfectly designed to achieve what we are currently achieving." If we make application of this statement to the church today, one of the questions we might ask would be: Are we satisfied with what we are currently achieving? In other words, are we content or pleased with the impact the church is having today? If we are totally honest, the answer would seem to be a resounding *no*.

The fact is, regardless of what marker a person looks at to judge the health of the church in North America, every indicator is trending in the wrong direction. If we are perfectly designed to achieve what the church is currently achieving, then shouldn't we ask if there is an issue in the way we are designed? Or at least question if there is an issue in the way we understand the nature of the church and its place in God's mission? Are there "design" factors that we need to rethink to achieve the outcomes we desire?

Part of the solution is found in rethinking the nature of the church, mission, discipleship, evangelism and vocation, along with several other aspects of the life of the church. In this chapter, I want to suggest that there is also an organizational issue that needs to be addressed that relates to how you form your church planting team and how to activate every member of the church plant.

CLERGY-LAITY DIVIDE

Before addressing a specific way to look at the gifting and functions of the body of Christ, let's consider a general view of leadership that in many ways has kept the church from fully realizing its calling. It is referred to as the clergy-laity divide.

The word *laity* comes from a Greek word (*laos*) that means *people*. Today we often use the related term *layperson* in distinction from the word *professional*. A layperson is someone in a particular discipline who is seen as an amateur—someone who dabbles in a certain area but doesn't operate with a high level of skill or expertise. The professional, on the other hand, is the expert. He is the one in the know. She has the expertise to operate at a high level. While there may be a place for this division in the business world or the area of sports, there is no biblical basis for such a distinction in the church. Eugene Peterson writes on the insidious nature of such language.

> *Within the Christian community there are few words that are more disabling than layperson and laity. The words convey the impression—an impression that quickly solidifies into a lie—that there is a two-level hierarchy among the men and women who follow Jesus. There are those who are trained, sometimes referred to as "the called," the professionals who are paid to preach, teach, and provide guidance in the Christian way, occupying the upper level. The lower level is made up of everyone else, those whom God assigned jobs as storekeepers, lawyers, journalists, parents and computer programmers.[83]*

In the New Testament, the word *laos* literally means *the people of God*. The *laos*, or laity, are the whole people of God together who are called to *be* the church. Ministry, therefore, is not set aside for some professional class within the church, but instead all the people of God are called and commissioned. In the classic book, *The Community of the King*, author Howard Snyder speaks to this issue.

> *The New Testament doctrine of ministry rests not on the clergy-laity distinction but on the twin and complementary pillars of the priesthood of all believers and the gifts of the Spirit. To-day, four centuries after the Reformation, the full implications of this Protestant affirmation have yet to be worked out. The clergy-laity dichotomy is a direct carry-over from pre-Reformation Roman Catholicism and a throwback to the Old Testament priesthood. It is one of the principal obstacles to the church effectively being God's agent of the Kingdom today because it creates a false idea that only "holy men," namely, ordained ministers, are really qualified and responsible for leadership and significant ministry. In the New Testament there are functional distinctions between various kinds of ministries but no hierarchical division between clergy and laity.[84]*

We need to "de-professionalize" ministry and give it back to the people of God. However, this does not mean we don't have leaders. Any significant movement that makes an impact has definite leadership. We simply shouldn't confuse leadership with ministry. Not all are leaders, but all are ministers.[85]

Ephesians 4 tells us that when all the members (*laos* = people of God) are properly working together, the body grows up into maturity, to the stature of the fullness of Christ (4:15). Such maturity is not possible if only 10 percent of the body exercises their calling. Fullness will be found when the other 90 percent activate their gifting.

When we look at the early church (and every other Jesus movement throughout history), we see that every member of the body of Christ is regarded as a significant agent of the King and is encouraged to find their place in the unfolding of the movement. In other words, in the church that Jesus built, everyone gets to play. In fact, everyone must play!

THE IMPORTANCE OF APEST

Now that we have made the case for activating all the people of God, let's move to a specific way to accomplish the task. Part of the solution of diminishing the clergy-laity divide and helping the *laos* engage in mission and ministry involves broadening our concept of ministry. We need to move beyond ministry being framed simply by the traditional pastor-teacher model of the church to a fivefold understanding of ministry giftings, or functions, as described in Ephesians 4:1-16. This fivefold framework is often referred to as APEST: Apostle, Prophet, Evangelist, Shepherd and Teacher. Expanding our application of the Ephesians 4 passage does *not* diminish the irreplaceable roles shepherds and teachers play in the life of the church, but it does, or should, expand our view of ministry and help the church engage God's mission more fully.

Let's begin by examining the Ephesians 4 passage. But before reading the text, consider a rarely discussed aspect of this passage. In the vast majority of cases, the church has read this passage as a leadership text. In other words, we normally understand the gifts that are mentioned as leaders given to the church for the purpose of equipping the rest of the people of God. They have been seen more as roles than functions. However, one of the most revolutionary aspects of Ephesians 4 is that it is not a leadership text—it is a text about the ministry of the church. Rather than a leadership text, it is a body of Christ text. Paul is stating that the gifts given to the church are actually given to the *laos*—the whole people of God.

> *As a prisoner for the Lord, then, I urge you to live a life worthy of the calling you have received. Be completely humble and gentle; be patient, bearing with one another in love. Make every effort to keep the unity of the Spirit through the bond of peace. There is one body and one Spirit, just as you were called to one hope when you were called; one Lord, one faith, one baptism; one God and Father of all, who is over all and through all and in all.*
>
> *But to each one of us grace has been given as Christ apportioned it. This is why it says: "When he ascended on high, he took many captives and gave gifts to his people." (What does "he ascended" mean except that he also descended to the lower, earthly regions? He who descended is the very one who ascended higher than all the heavens, in order to fill the whole universe.) So, Christ himself gave the apostles, the prophets, the evangelists, the pastors and teachers, to equip his people for works of service, so that the body of Christ may be built up until we all reach unity in the faith and in the knowledge of the Son of God and become mature, attaining to the whole measure of the fullness of Christ.*
>
> *Then we will no longer be infants, tossed back and forth by the waves, and blown here and there by every wind of teaching and by the cunning and craftiness of people in their deceitful scheming. Instead, speaking the truth in love, we will grow to become in every respect the mature body of*

> *him who is the head, that is, Christ. From him the whole body, joined and held together by every supporting ligament, grows and builds itself up in love, as each part does its work. (Ephesians 4:1-16, NIV)*

The first thing to keep in mind is that Paul is giving us his best thinking about the nature and function of the church. At the heart of his letter, here in Ephesians 4, is his understanding and description of the essential ministry of the church. Paul presents us with the logic of the church's ministry. Consider it this way:

- In verses 1–6, Paul calls us to realize and live out our fundamental unity in the one God.
- In verses 7–11, he says that APEST has been given to the church by Christ.
- In verses 12–16, he says why APEST is given, so that we might be built up, reach unity and become mature.

Paul is outlining the core ministries that make up the body of Christ. He clearly states that Christ has given certain gifts to "each one of us" and distributed them throughout the body as He sees fit. The ministry of the church is unmistakably stated as being at least fivefold in form.[86] This fivefold form finds expression in the giftings of apostle, prophet, evangelist, shepherd and teacher. And it is through the diversity of APEST that the church is able to operate in the fullness of Christ's ministry.

The word *equip* (v. 12) in this passage is an interesting word. It was often used to describe the setting of a broken bone (alignment). Paul is saying that each of the ministries within APEST somehow adds capacity to the rest of the body and helps it function properly. Our ability to grow and mature into the church that Jesus intended us to be is directly linked to all the ministries within APEST.

Unfortunately, most churches have traditionally operated with only two out of the five: namely shepherding and teaching. In most cases, the ministries of the apostle, prophet and evangelist (APEs) have often been minimized, if not completely relegated, out of the vocabulary and ministry of the church. According to Ephesians 4, we essentially cut off three-fifths of our capacity to grow and mature as the body of Christ, which has done serious damage to the church's ability to be the fullness of Christ in the world.

Before examining each of the Ephesian 4 gifts more closely, let us make a point of clarification. Often people will ask how the APEST gifts differ from gifts listed in other New Testament passages, namely 1 Corinthians 12 and Romans 12. One helpful distinction is that each gift list is preceded by a particular word that helps us understand each unique list.

The keyword in 1 Corinthians 12 is *manifestation*. This list of gifts, given by the Spirit, manifests the power of the Spirit through the giving of gifts like healing, speaking in tongues, faith and miracles. The keyword in Romans 12 is *praxis*, because these are action-oriented skills. The keyword for the Ephesians 4 list is *calling* (4:1), because these are *people* gifts, or we might use the word *vocational* gifts. (Remember, vocation means *calling*.) The gifts in 1 Corinthians 12 and Romans 12 are gifts given to us personally, while in Ephesians 4 the people themselves are the gift. "We find our calling in the fivefold typology, and the other gifts are given to us by God to enable us to live out our vocation."[87]

APEST SUMMARY

To gain a better understanding of each of the gifts/functions mentioned in Ephesians 4, here is a brief summary.[88]

The Apostle

"One who is sent and extends"

The word *apostle* literally means *sent one*. The Latin form of this word is *missio*, which is where we get our English word *mission*. The apostle is the one most responsible to activate, develop and protect the missionary "sentness" of the church. This sent quality gives the apostle's life a catalytic influence, often playing the role of entrepreneur at the forefront of new ventures. They are cultural architects who are concerned with the overall extension of Christianity as a whole throughout culture and society. As such, they are often drawn to issues related to design, systems and overarching organizational structures. Above all, they have a missional (sent) focus to their ministry.

The Prophet
"One who questions and reforms"

Prophets are sensitive to God and what is important to Him. They often have a sense of what truth needs to be emphasized for their time and place. Essentially, prophets are guardians of the covenant relationship. Whether it is in the church, society or some organizational setting, prophets are quick to recognize the gap between "what is" and "what should be." The weight of this tension leads prophets to question the status quo as well as initiate efforts of re- form. Ultimately, they are not satisfied until they see a closing of the gap between God's demands and our covenantal faithfulness. This desire to see the truth of God's reality fleshed out in concrete and tangible ways gives an incarnational quality to their ministry.

The Evangelist
"One who recruits and gathers"

Evangelists communicate the message of the Good News in joyous, infectious ways. They tend to enjoy meeting new people and wooing them into a relationship. They are avid communicators of ideas and often share their thoughts and feelings in convincing ways. They are recruiters to the cause and find great fulfillment in helping people get caught up into the driving narrative of the church/organization—the gospel of the kingdom. As people who are bearers of good news, they have an attractional quality to their ministry.

The Shepherd
"One who protects and provides"

Shepherds have a natural instinct to protect the community from danger and provide for its needs on both an individual and communal level. They often notice when people are alone or hurting and feel drawn to nurture the spiritual and communal health of the church. They have a sense of loyalty to the organization and the people within it. They ensure the community is experienced as a safe and loving environment, giving their ministry a distinctly communal focus.

The Teacher
"One who understands and explains"

Teachers find great satisfaction in helping people learn truth and wisdom. As the more philosophical types, they grasp complex, systemic truths and then help people understand them. They often formulate curriculum and pathways of learning. They ensure the truths of Scripture are passed along from generation to generation. Their ministry could be said to be primarily instructional in nature.

FULLY FUNCTIONING AS THE BODY OF CHRIST

Having given some definition to the various APEST ministries, we can now see the spiritual power of these as they are brought together in the church. It is hard to see how we could possibly thrive, with- out a fivefold APEST ministry.

In fact, serious dysfunction will inevitably occur when one form of ministry becomes dominant. This is because one form cannot possibly represent the whole ministry of Christ in the world. For example, when one form of APEST leadership is dislocated from the others, it will tend to monopolize the culture and have a negative effect in the long run. The one-leader type of church is most at risk in this case, but we can recall organizations that demonstrate the truth of this. For instance:

A/PEST: If an apostolic leader dominates, the church or other organization will tend to be hard-driving, dictatorial, with lots of pressure for change and development and will leave lots of wounded people in its wake. It simply is not sustainable.

P/AEST: If the prophetic leader dominates, the organization will be one-dimensional (usually harking back to one or two issues), will likely be factious and sectarian, will have a "super spiritual" vibe, or, somewhat paradoxically, will tend to be either too activist to be sustainable or too perfectionist to be useful. This is not a viable form of organization.

E/~~APST~~: When an evangelistic leader dominates, the organization will be obsessed with numerical growth, will often create dependence on charismatic leadership and will tend to lack theological breadth and depth. This type of organization will not empower many people.

S/<u>APET</u>: When pastoral leadership monopolizes, the church or other organization will tend to be risk-averse, codependent and needy, and overly lacking in healthy dissent and, therefore, creativity. Such an organization will lack innovation and will not be able to transfer its core message and tasks from one generation to the next.

T/~~APES~~: When teachers and theologians rule, the church will be ideological, controlling and somewhat moralistic. A rationalistic, doctrine-obsessed Christian Gnosticism (the idea that we are saved by what we know) will tend to replace reliance on the Holy Spirit. These types of organization will be exclusively based on ideology.

A church plant that can bring together, encourage and capture the gifting of a *fully functioning team* will succeed in whatever it is seeking to achieve. Each of the APEST vocations adds an absolutely necessary ingredient to the overall missional fitness and maturity of the church. Further, it is crucial to understand that each vocation needs to be informed and shaped by the others in order to anchor the church in the fullness of Christ's nature and mission.

FINAL THOUGHT ON APEST AND THE ORDER OF CREATION

When articulating APEST to your church planting team, it may be helpful to recognize that the fivefold callings are not only exhibited in the person of Jesus and reflected in the functions of the church, but they are also seen in the order of creation. In other words, these apply in some way to all people, not just Christians. In the book *The*

Permanent Revolution, author Alan Hirsch contends that we can interpret society in general through the APEST grid:[89]

- Apostles in the generic sense are those sent to pioneer some- thing new—for example, teachers who are called in to turn failing schools around, along with people who start movements of sorts, architect systems or entrepreneurial business ventures. Can we see non-Christian people who fit this category? Definitely.
- Prophets tend to be visionaries, but in a very different sense, they often have a keen interest in issues of justice, environmental responsibility or the creative arts. Are there such people outside the church? Of course.
- Evangelists are particularly gifted at enthusing others about what they stand for, selling the significance of their work, company or product outside the group itself. These are easy to spot. The United States is full of them.
- Pastors/shepherds are those with a special concern for seeing and affirming what is human within structures. They might not be the most appropriate people to put together a policy for addressing drug abuse, but if they are not part of delivering the policy, the addicts are in trouble. Are there people who create community and bring healing to others in the non-Christian world? Indeed.
- Teachers are those who are effective trainers and inspirers of learning. They are philosophers, thinkers and people who understand ideas and how they shape human life. Do such non-Christians exist? No brainer.

Viewing APEST sociologically allows us, in at least some sense, to demystify the language of fivefold. When we see it this way, we can see how deeply rooted they are in creation, but also how powerful these roles really are.

Any healthy leadership team in any context (corporate, non-profit or anything else) would benefit from such a complex of influences. It also gives us insight into why having only two of the types in the mix leads to dysfunctions. Finally, it is very helpful because it helps us to appreciate the sheer movement power of the redemption won in and through Jesus Christ. People who are naturally inclined to one of the other APEST types are redeemed, set apart, focused and legitimized in the church. In fact, they are Christ's ascension gifts (Ephesians 4:8-10).[90]

ACTION

1. To better understand your own gifting regarding APEST, take the personal profile assessment. You can find that test here: http://5qcentral.com/tests
2. If you already have a church planting team in place, have each member take the assessment. After every person has received his or her results, make time to discuss, with special emphasis on team dynamics.
3. If your current church plant team does not reflect a fully functioning APEST team, 1) identify which gifts are you missing, and 2) list those whom you may equip or recruit to create a five-fold team.

REFLECTION

1. Which one of the five APEST ministry roles is easiest for you to associate with Jesus? Which is the most difficult to associate with Him?
2. What do you think could happen if the people in your city caught a glimpse of a church that represented the entire spectrum of Christ's ministry contained within APEST? How do you think their view of Christ and His church would change? What would they see? Would there be a sense of awe? What would impact them most?
3. These giftings, as mentioned before, are not just given to leaders. They are given to each one of us. How does this change the way you see your role in the body of Christ?

4. If God were to use your team to start a movement in your city, what do you think it would look like? Describe some of the things that would be different if your church had a revolutionary impact in your city.
5. Why is it important to recognize that the APEST giftings have been given to the entire body of Christ and not just a group of leaders? How will you begin to identify, equip and release all the gifts in your church plant?

CHAPTER EIGHTEEN

MOVEMENT AND MULTIPLICATION

Movement occurs when the making of mission-shaped disciples—who live in the world for the sake of the world, in the way of Christ—goes viral.

– J.R. Woodward

Movements are more like starfish than they are spiders. You can kill a spider by taking its head off. Spiders have a centralized control center. On the other hand, when a starfish is cut up, it will produce more starfish. Each part carries the potential for the whole.

– Alan Hirsch

RETHINK

In a blog post on church planting movements, Ed Stetzer challenged his readers to compare the pregnancies of elephants and rabbits.

> *Elephants have the longest gestation period in nature. After getting pregnant, a female elephant will carry her calf inside of her for nearly two full years! It's almost unheard of for more than one*

calf to be born at a time. Upon birth, the calf is able to immediately stand up on his or her feet and walk a few steps. This 260-pound "baby" will feed on his or her mother's milk for about six months. At that point, the calf will begin transitioning to solid food, while continuing to nurse until age three. This whole cycle won't start again for the mother until her calf is fully weaned. And for the calf, it will take 15 years before he or she begins his or her own reproductive life.

Let's now take a look at the reproductive life-cycle of a rabbit. The gestation period for a rabbit is usually a month. At birth, a single female rabbit will typically expect not one, but up to 14 babies per litter. Within minutes after giving birth, it's possible for a female rabbit to be impregnated again. That means a female rabbit can potentially have one litter per month! And as early as six months into their life, rabbits will begin reproducing.

Let's just take a moment and do the math. If a rabbit has an average of three female babies per litter per month, then at the end of year one, there will be 37 female rabbits (including the mother). If all 37 reproduce at the same rate, then at the end of year two, there will be a total of 1,369 female rabbits (including the original 37). At the end of year three, it jumps to 50,653 and so on and so on.

Compare that to elephants. At the end of year one, there's only one, as the calf is still in the mother. At the end of year two, there are now two elephants: the mother and the calf. At the end of year three, there are still two. If the female elephant gets impregnated after weaning her calf at the end of year three, then it wouldn't be until year five that the number of elephants jumps to an astronomically high number—three.

> *While there is definitely still a place for lengthy, elephant-like approaches to church planting, if we want to see movements of churches that birth 1,000 each in their lifetime, then we need to "breed like rabbits."*[91]

MOVEMENT IS A MINDSET

Perhaps the very first thing that should be said regarding church planting and movements is that it must be a mindset. We need to have a rabbit kind of mentality that will not only change the way we think about church, mission and multiplication, but will begin to shape the very way we function as the church. Rather than an alternative model of doing church, it is a complete paradigm shift in the way we think.

Albert Einstein's saying is correct as we apply it to the church in North America: We cannot solve the problems of the church by using the same kind of thinking we used when we created those problems in the first place. In other words, we can't keep thinking and doing what we have already done and expect different results. We must thoroughly reimagine how we understand and live out the life of the church if we wish to truly see a movement.

Make it a discipline to think *movements*, not *institutions*. If you identify yourself as a movement, and take it seriously, you will eventually start acting like one.

THE MAKEUP OF A MOVEMENT

What are the tangible characteristics of multiplying churches that are attempting to live out a movement ethos? Here are four aspects that help to make up a movement culture.

1. GOD'S MISSION IS CENTRAL

A church that is focused on real movement has a strong emphasis on the *missio Dei*. It is God who has a mission to set things right in a broken, sinful world to redeem and restore it to what He has always intended.

A movement church will understand that mission is not the invention, responsibility or program of the church. Instead, they will see that mission flows directly from the character and purposes of a missionary God. In the words of South African missiologist David Bosch, "It is not the church which undertakes mission; it is the *missio Dei* which constitutes the church." Or stated in a slightly different way, "It is not so much that God has a mission for His church in the world, but that God has a church for His mission in the world."

A movement church will not only understand that the mission is God's, but they will also recognize that His mission is larger than their particular church. They will live out the reality that God's primary activity is in the world, and their responsibility is to be *sent* into the world to participate in what He is already doing. As a result, the church will not simply *send* missionaries, instead they view their church *as* the missionary.

2. ALL OF GOD'S PEOPLE ARE ACTIVATED

Movements only succeed to the degree that they legitimize and activate the ministry of *all* of God's people. Every believer carries within him or her the potential for world transformation. Consider this: In every seed is the potential for a tree, and in every tree the potential for a forest, but all of this is contained in the initial seed. In every spark, there is a potential for a flame, and in every flame is the potential for fire, but all of this is potentially contained in the originating spark.[92]

All the potential for movement is already present in God's people; our job as church leaders is to bring it out. In a movement church, everyone gets to play! No one sits on the bench.

3. ADAPTIVE LEADERSHIP AND ADAPTIVE STRUCTURES

A movement church has the kind of leadership that knows how to move a church and keep it moving. As discussed in the last chapter on APEST, this type of leadership highlights the apostolic and prophetic roles. The prophetic person will tend to call the status quo into question, while the apostolic leads with a positive vision of what can be.

What Western Christianity desperately needs now is adaptive leadership—people who can help the church transition to a different, nimbler mode of church. Such leaders don't necessarily have to be highly creative innovators themselves, but they must be people who can move the church into adaptive modes—people who can create the conditions for change and innovation.

Adaptive challenges include the kind of work more typical to church planting. Things like cultivating, growing and reproducing healthy communities, the work of racial reconciliation in a given neighborhood, and leadership development of younger Christians are all adaptive challenges. These types of challenges are rarely accomplished with a linear, step-by-step approach. Though they might include some technical components within them, the larger adaptive challenge is only solved through a process undertaken by a group of people having various roles.

In movement-focused churches, the effectiveness of the leaders is not measured by what they do or do not accomplish, but by how the people of God are equipped, enabled, organized and inspired to participate in God's mission in the world. The church today needs leaders who can model a kind of spirituality that doesn't reject the rebels and risk takers in the church, but instead listens, discerns and validates their necessary perspective and then releases them into their calling.

Further, in a movement church, the leadership and structure are geared toward disciple making. In the makeup of a movement, discipleship is the engine for everything. Without it, the church will drift away from its core calling.

Movement occurs when the making of mission-shaped disciples—who live in the world for the sake of the world in the way of Christ—goes viral. Movement is about developing structures and systems that catapult people into mission, where reproducing discipleship groups, missional communities, churches and networks of churches is a natural part of its DNA. It's the ripple effect: throwing a rock into a pond creates one ripple and then another and another, till ripples cover the whole pond.[93]

4. APEST WITH AN EMPHASIS ON THE A

While all five APEST ministries have a role that is vital and nonnegotiable, the apostolic in particular is the key to a movement—the kind we see on the pages of the New Testament. This is not an emphasis of importance or priority; it is one of purpose and design. By nature and calling, the apostolic person (the sent one) follows the inherent impulses of his or her sentness and pushes the organization to the edge in order to establish Christianity upon new ground. The pattern is clear: Remove apostolic influences, and you won't get apostolic movement.[94]

MOVEMENT HEROES

One last thought on creating a movement culture. Our heroes are those people in our world who demonstrate through their lives what we think is truly valuable. They live out what we all hope to be. Heroes and their stories inspire us because they reach into, and embody, the vision of what we want to be and become.

For example, if your church's hero is a brilliant scholar or preacher, then everyone gets the message that it is scholarship and preaching that are most prized. If, on the other hand, the church's hero is the church planter or pioneer who is leading the charge to start new things to impact society, then people get the message that missional-incarnational mission is highly valued. The same is true for advocates of racial reconciliation, justice and so on. The heroes we champion are the living examples of what we are seeking to achieve. Don't underestimate the importance of everyday heroes—they are embodiments of change.[95]

ACTION

1. Review each of the four "The Makeup of Movement" characteristics. Identify at least one thing from each of the movement ideas that you can do to implement movement thinking into your church plant.

2. Identify the heroes that you and your church champion. What do they communicate about what the church values?

REFLECTION

1. What does it mean to have a movement mentality?
2. What are the biggest differences you see between the church as a movement and the church as an institution?
3. What is the first step for *you* to take to live out the church as a movement?

CHAPTER NINETEEN

CREATING NEW SCORECARDS

Measurement is fabulous. Unless you're busy measuring what's easy to measure as opposed to what's important.

– Seth Godin

RETHINK

When it comes to keeping score, churches in North America have typically focused on three metrics: buildings, budgets and butts. While there is nothing inherently wrong with counting each of these things, we do need to ask if keeping score of how big our buildings are, how much money people give and how many show up when we meet is the best indicator of how a church is doing?

The fact is these three metrics really give us no real sense on the influence a church is having on its community. Do the number of people who attend a Sunday morning gathering give you any indication of the impact the church is having on an individual neighborhood or the city as a whole? The answer has to be a resounding NO! There is *absolutely* no correlation between the number of people who show up for an event and the difference those people are having where they live. The same is true with how much money people give to the church and how large a church's buildings are. We count those three things because they are easy to count. But we must be challenged to not *count* what is easy, but instead *measure* what is important.

COUNTING (QUANTITATIVE) AND MEASURING (QUALITATIVE)

While we often use the language of counting and measuring inter- changeably, there is actually a difference between the two. It is important to make the distinction because the church has largely been in the counting business, which has negatively influenced the way we think about the nature of the church and limited our impact in the world. We need to move to measuring more and counting less. Let's make the distinction this way:

Counting is giving attention to numbers. When counting, the question to be answered is: "How many?" It is quantitative. Conversations about "How many?" are most frequently conversations about resources but can also be about activities. Conversations about resources in a time of limited resources are commonly conversations about sufficiency, "Do we have enough?" or, "How can we get more?" Examples could include finances or people. We ask questions like, "Do we have enough money for that mission?" or "Do we have enough volunteers for that ministry?" A quantitative question about activities might be, "How many Bible studies were conducted?"[96]

Measuring is giving attention to change. When measuring, the question is not about "How many?" but rather about "How far?" Conversations about "How far?" are frequently about the change that can be measured over a particular time, as in, "How far have we come over the past year?" Measuring is about qualitative change. Has the quality of something changed over time? In other words, has something gotten better or worse since the last time we measured?

There is, of course, a need for both counting and measuring. In all complex organizations, multiple tools are needed. However, like all tools the right tool must be chosen for the job at hand. So, what sorts of things should we count? And what should we measure?

I hesitate to be too prescriptive in giving suggestions for what your church plant could count and measure because contexts are different. But let me suggest some possibilities that will hopefully crack open your imagination for metrics that fit your community more specifically.

COUNTING

Because the church is a missionary entity—we are the sent, missionary people of God—one of the things we should count are missionary behaviors. You should be asking and counting things like: How many neighbors have I gotten to know by name in the past month? How many coworkers have I gotten to know on a deeper level? How many significant conversations have I had in my favorite Third Place? How many people have I had in my home this past month? How many meals have I shared with people outside my church family this week? How many times this week have I intentionally been a blessing to someone?

Not only does counting the right things give us a better indication of a church's engagement in the community, and ultimately its impact, but it also illustrates to the congregation what is important. The reality is what gets measured gets done *and* what gets measured gets repeated.

In the book *Missional Renaissance: Changing the Scorecard for the Church*, author Reggie McNeal suggests developing new scorecards around six resources of the church: prayer, people, time, finances, facilities and technology. Here are just a few ideas of questions in each of those categories that will help move the church to think outside the church walls:

PRAYER

- Number of specific people being prayed for both inside and outside the church
- Number of people prayed with during the week by church members
- Number of prayer meetings conducted off church property

- Number of community leaders adopted and prayed for each week
- Number of prayer-walks taken in the community/neighborhoods
- Number of prayer cards received from community prayer boxes
- Time spent in prayer in staff meetings for community needs
- Number of times each week schoolteachers are prayed for/over

PEOPLE

- Number of people engaged in financial planning
- Number of people growing in financial giving to kingdom causes
- Number of people engaged in daily spiritual formation
- Number of people pursuing an intentional learning agenda
- Number of people reporting increased friendships over time
- Number of people sent into trailer parks, apartments, retirement centers
- Number of community ministries adopted by church groups/classes
- Number of people serving other people in some venue
- Number of people serving as mentors
- Number of people practicing intentional blessing strategy

TIME AND CALENDAR

- Amount of time spent debriefing people engaged in community service
- Time spent in mentoring people in the community beyond the church
- Number of hours people spend in direct ministry to community needs
- Amount of time spent in gatherings celebrating stories of community involvement
- Hours spent each week building relationships in Third Places

- Number of hours each week members open their homes to others
- Hours each week spent supporting/ministering to single parents
- Amount of time staff spends developing relationships with community leaders

FINANCES
- Number of people reporting personal debt retirement
- Number of people increasing in their generosity through charitable giving
- Number of people reporting they have developed a personal budget
- Percent of church budget moving toward externally focused ministry
- Reduction of church debt to free up dollars for people investment
- Amount of money invested in microeconomic development

FACILITIES
- Number of schools using the church facilities for their activities
- Number of community organizations using the church facilities (Big Brothers, Boy Scouts, AA, other churches)
- Space devoted to conversation-friendly areas
- Use of church land for soccer/baseball fields, basketball court, skateboard park
- Number of hours the facilities are used during the week by people for personal growth such as exercise classes, tutoring, life skill seminars, etc.

TECHNOLOGY
- Number of podcast interviews with community leaders
- Space on church website dedicated to community events and engagement

- Number of webinars to educate people of missional opportunities
- Number of graphics or videos telling the stories of missional engagement by members

Not only does counting the right things give us a better indication of a church's engagement in the community, and ultimately its impact, but it also illustrates to the congregation what is important. The reality is what gets measured gets done *and* what gets measured gets repeated. When we count the things suggested in the above list, people know what is valued; they, therefore, know the target for which they need to be aiming.

MEASURING

While all the suggestions listed can certainly help a church begin to move in the right direction, these questions are still about *activities*. They are more about inputs rather than outcomes. It is important to say that again. They are more about inputs, rather than outcomes. Unfortunately, most often in the nonprofit church world, we stop with inputs.[97]

What is meant by measurables that are outcome-based? First, they are primarily about change. If we can describe the change we desire to see or make, then we can also have conversations about whether we are moving toward that change over time. Measuring relates not so much to what *is*, but rather what *could be*. It is more about possibilities.

Second, the best questions associated with measuring ask about both change and time. For example, we might ask, "How have the test scores changed over the past six months in the elementary school where the church provides tutors?"

In the context of the church, measuring is about determining transformational change (discipleship) in both people and in the neighborhoods where we live. Ask yourself, "What changes would you like to see in the lives of the people, but also in the life of your community?" That is an outcome.

But then ask the follow-up question, "What will it take to get to that place?" Then begin to ask measurement questions toward that change. "How will we know if we are making progress in the right direction?" "What will we measure to determine transformational change?" Measuring is *definitely* more difficult than counting, but in almost every single case, it is essential if we are serious about making a difference.

ACTION

1. Articulate in your own words the difference between *counting* and *measuring*.
2. Create your own scorecard that reflects the need to both count and measure. Either build your own list or choose some from this chapter that would fit your context.

REFLECTION

1. What are your thoughts on the suggestion that the typical counting of buildings, budgets and butts is a poor indicator of the effectiveness of a church? Is that a fair assessment?
2. What things do you presently count and/or measure in your church plant? After engaging this chapter, are you reconsidering how you keep score?
3. Which of the questions from the prayer, people, time, finances, facilities and technology list stand out for you? Which would be a good fit for your church? What other questions come to mind in each of these categories?

SECTION FIVE

SUSTAINABLE LIFE

CHAPTER TWENTY

COVO APTITUDES

The one who is wise, therefore, will see their life as more like a reservoir than a canal. The canal simultaneously pours out what it receives; the reservoir retains the water till it is filled, then discharges the overflow without loss to itself… Today there are many in the Church who act like canals, the reservoirs are far too rare…They want to pour forth before they have been filled; they are more ready to speak than to listen, impatient to teach what they have not grasped, and full of presumption to govern others while they know not how to govern themselves.

– Bernard of Clairvaux

Hurried leaders are quick to do and slow to be; quick to speak but slow to listen; quick to teach and slow to learn; quick to lead others but slow to let God lead them beside his still waters.

– Alan Fadling

If you are tuned out of your own emotions, you will be poor at reading them in other people.

– Daniel Goleman

RETHINK

To introduce this last section of the book titled *Sustainable Life*, I want to introduce you to a way to frame your aptitude for bivo or covocational church planting. In the book *BiVO: A Modern-Day Guide for Bi-Vocational Saints*, author Hugh Halter shares six "knacks" that he believes a planter needs to consider before deciding to plant bivocationally. He uses the term *knack* because it communicates a growing aptitude—not perfection. It simply means that you are developing the knack for something specific. Below is a short description of each of the knacks.[98]

PERSONAL KNACK

The ability to own one's life. This category assesses personal ownership, motivation, discipline, physical health, optimism, fortitude, work ethic, the ability to multitask, and the discipline to plan and schedule time. Essentially one's personal knack is the ability to manage yourself.

FAMILY KNACK

This assesses for spousal buy-in, spousal cohesion, strength of marriage and the emotional depth of parent-to-child relationship. Essentially, the family knack is the strength and stability of your family to move into mission together.

RELATIONAL KNACK

This knack assesses incarnational aptitude, street cred with people, likability, the ability to draw people, energy for humans, network capacity in community and ability to lead community. Essentially, this knack is about whether or not people will want to follow you and be with you and whether or not you will be able to give this level of relational time to people.

SPIRITUAL KNACK

This assesses your spiritual stability—whether you are clear on identity in Christ, your level of pride and humility, your ability to hear and follow God's voice, and your ability to walk by faith. Essentially the spiritual knack is about truly walking with God and letting Him lead on an hourly/daily basis.

FINANCIAL KNACK

This assesses the level of desperation versus stability with money, self-control, living by budget, generosity and ability to handle stress together as a couple. This also assesses what you have to work with or what God has given you to steward—your actual cash reality and potential, as well as your assets that can be used for kingdom purposes, such as house, yard, business office space, other stuff, etc. Essentially this knack is about how well-positioned you are to live bivocationally.

SKILL KNACK

This assesses for clarity and creativeness on your specific skills, gifts and spiritual gifts that God can use. It includes your network position in the neighborhood or business, how you lead best, as well as your personality style. Essentially, this knack is about how God will use you in the world.

After giving a brief overview of a few of the special knacks that are necessary to successfully manage a bivo or covo life, let's move to discuss three key aptitudes in greater detail.

BIVO/COVO APTITUDE: PERSONAL MANAGEMENT

Perhaps one of the most significant topics when it comes to managing ourselves is the issue of time. Following is a simple, yet helpful, way to organize your week based on the illustration where you fill a jar with big rocks first, then medium-sized rocks and finally let God fill in all the cracks and crevices.

BIG ROCKS: THE "HAVE- TOS" AND "GET-TOS"

Sabbath: The more you learn about the orientation of Jesus to the Father, the more you come to realize that God wants us to prioritize an abiding life with Him first and then let our work-flow from that. Most of us work frantically trying to juggle life, hoping that God will lead us and bless us, but the truth of Scripture and the teaching of the Sabbath is that God blesses and favors those who make sure they rest and abide first and then let God build influence from their work. Your physical well-being, mental stability and overall soul care are the deep wells of good news you give to people, so it makes sense that you prioritize this side of life.[99]

Read the two quotes at the beginning of this lesson from Bernard of Clairvaux and Alan Fadling. Are you more of a reservoir or a canal? Do you find yourself wanting to "pour forth" before being filled up? Would you consider yourself a hurried leader? We must recognize that everything starts there. Having time for all the other important aspects of life, ministry and mission has to flow out of our time with the Father.

Family time: While your Sabbath time may include this, make sure you also schedule in the family time as a "big rock." This may involve time watching kids' athletic and extracurricular school activities, games, plays, etc. Also, schedule in family nights and dates with your spouse.

Vacation: Even if some of your vacations are "staycations," there must be extended times scheduled as "big rocks" where you completely unplug from the normal rhythms of work.

MEDIUM ROCKS: "SHOULD-DOS"

Time with Leaders: As an equipper, you need to give your best time to your best leaders. If they do well, your entire movement does well.

Time with Lost People: Your next time commitment should be with those who do not know Christ. If church planting is truly about impacting lostness and transforming your community, then, as followers of Jesus, we need to be the advocate of lost people. This means we will spend coffee times, mealtimes, workout times, etc., in pre-conversion discipling relationships.

LITTLE ROCKS: "GOD-GETS-TOS"

Space: Blocking out space or undesignated time is critical for spontaneous ministry to happen. In the next chapter, we will discuss the topic of margin. Margin is the space between our load and our limits, between vitality and fatigue. It is the opposite of overload. The fact is that relationships happen in the margins. In other words, if we never block out time for God to spontaneously interrupt us for His purposes, we will miss wonderful opportunities to join Him in what He is already doing.

Church Stuff: The last things are the activities you must do to help the broader movement. That could be a few hours for sermon prep, two hours for staff time, a quarterly leader training, etc. As a covocational leader, you will discover that many gathered church activities don't take (or shouldn't take) as much planning time as we have been led to believe.

BIVO/COVO APTITUDE: RELATIONAL MANAGEMENT

Much of the leadership training and seminars today focus on developing management skills. Ministry, however, is not about tasks. Ministry is about people. The Great Commission centers upon making disciples, and to do that a leader must make human beings his textbook. One of the key bivocational aptitudes is the ability to manage relationships. It is crucial to success because so much of what we do has a relational component.

UNDERSTANDING YOURSELF

One of the keys to relational management is to be able to understand the relationship you have to yourself. Mastering your own emotions and being able to interact with others in a controlled, empathetic manner is known as emotional intelligence, or EQ for short. *Psychology Today* offers the following definition of EQ:

> *Emotional intelligence is the ability to identify and manage your own emotions and the emotions of others. It is generally said to include three skills:*

1. Emotional awareness, including the ability to identify your own emotions and those of others; 2. The ability to harness emotions and apply them to tasks like thinking and problem solving; 3. The ability to manage emotions, including the ability to regulate your own emotions, and the ability to cheer up or calm down another person.

The New Testament gives counsel that aligns well with this understanding of EQ.

- Romans 12:15 urges us to "rejoice with those who rejoice, weep with those who weep" (ESV).
- James 1:19 instructs us to be "quick to listen, slow to speak and slow to become angry."
- First Thessalonians 5:11 tells us to "encourage one another and build one another up" (ESV).

Fundamental to a life of faith and ministry is other-centeredness. This is expressed by Paul in Philippians 2:3,4 this way, "do nothing from selfish ambition or conceit, but in humility consider others more significant than yourselves. Let each of you look not only to his own interests, but also to the interests of others" (ESV). When we live an other-centered life, we are practicing skills that improve our EQ. Studies have systematized the different categories of being relationally savvy, which help us identify areas where we need to improve our ability to empathize with others and respond appropriately.

However, while many Christian leaders focus on biblical knowledge and leadership skill, few give thought to their own emotional intelligence. Often the root cause of church conflict can be traced back to the lack of emotional maturity of a leader. Because many of those you will minister to in your church plant will be emotionally bruised on some level, it is crucial that you know how to be relationally savvy.

THE FIVE ELEMENTS OF EQ

There are five elements of emotional intelligence as defined by Daniel Goleman, an American psychologist who helped popularize the term[100]:

1. Self-awareness
2. Self-regulation
3. Motivation
4. Empathy
5. Social skills

Self-awareness includes being aware of the emotions inside you and how they affect the people around you. To develop in this category, the practice of journaling can help you get in touch with your emotions. Talking regularly with a friend may help if you are a verbal processor. We often go so fast in life that we manage tasks at breakneck speed and leave very little time to process, reflect or to critically think through things. Observing the ministry of Jesus is very informative on emotional intelligence, as Jesus often retreated alone to pray and talk things over with His Father when His minis- try had the potential to become overwhelming.

Self-regulation is the practice of feeling an emotion and not acting on it. Acting on an emotion rashly can have devastating effects on people around us and on our credibility as leaders. When James exhorts us to be slow to speak, he is urging that we bite our tongues and carve out time to process. Proverbs tells us that "a fool speaks all that is in his heart" (Proverbs 29:11). If you do not learn to control your own actions and tongue, people around you will eventually think you a fool. Further, when you don't control yourself as a leader, you cannot expect others around you to do likewise.

Motivation is the third component of EQ and will help the leader sort through why he is ministering in the first place. This component acts like a rudder and the sails in a ship. It helps focus us on the "why" of what we are doing.

Empathy is the ability to put yourself in the situations of others, including those who may disagree or even oppose you. Jesus clearly modeled empathy. He often delved into the heart of the issue and addressed the stimulus of the behavior, rather than the symptom.

The woman at the well had most likely been abandoned by five men, and Jesus tells her of a well of love that will never abandon her. Rather than addressing her red herring comments about worship, He focused on the deepest yearning of her heart. To do that, Jesus had to become a good listener, and John's gospel models Jesus as being an excellent conversationalist. To develop empathy, you must learn to listen to people carefully and make understanding your primary focus.

Social skills are the basic rules of engagement in our social settings. Developing these skills is crucial to building relationships. Much of what is considered a social skill is common sense and can be arrived at when the other four elements of emotional intelligence are developed. The problem is common sense isn't always common.

MODELING EMOTIONAL INTELLIGENCE

Learning to laugh at ourselves and not take ourselves so seriously is a massive step in beginning to address the real issues we have. It's actually the first step of emotional intelligence—being self-aware. If we cannot be honest with ourselves, then we cannot be honest with God. If we cannot be honest with God, then we become actors or hypocrites (literally "false faces"). The mask will only last so long in the sphere of public ministry. Dealing with people will eventually show who we truly are, and if we've not dealt with our feelings, we will not be in any shape to help other people deal with their own and develop more into the image of Jesus.

Jesus was the model of emotional intelligence. He did not suppress His anger but modeled self-restraint. Even in the cleansing of the temple, Jesus modeled controlled anger. He didn't fly into a blind rage as some have suggested. Instead, the Scripture tells us that He spent time weaving the cords together quietly before taking action. During that time, He was most likely sorting through His emotions and praying to His Father in heaven.

He didn't suppress negative emotions but clearly modeled how to act with an even-tempered, controlled anger. When Lazarus died, He wept. In the shadow of the cross, He was afraid. He despaired unto death. He longed to eat the Last Supper with them. He experienced frustration when asking, "O faithless generation, how long am I to be with you?" (Mark 9:19, ESV). He became exhausted, drained and spent, crashing in the bow of the boat moments after ministering. Jesus didn't pretend to be something he wasn't. Neither should any minister until he seeks to model what He was like.

Because you will be busy as a covocational church planter, it is important to stop and reflect regularly. This will be difficult, as you will feel the pull from multiple directions. However, to live a healthy, socially aware life, you will need to be able to carve out margin that allows time and space to reflect.

HOW TO IMPROVE YOUR EQ

The good news is that emotional intelligence can be learned and developed. As well as working on your skills in the five areas above, use these strategies:

- *Observe how you react to people.* Do you rush to judgment before you know all the facts? Do you stereotype? Look honestly at how you think and interact with other people. Try to put yourself in their place and be more open and accepting of their perspectives and needs.
- *Look at your work environment.* Do you seek attention for your accomplishments? Humility can be a wonderful quality, and it doesn't mean you're shy or lack self-confidence. When you practice humility, you say that you know what you did, and you can be quietly confident about it. Give others a chance to shine—put the focus on them, and don't worry too much about getting praise for yourself.
- *Do a self-evaluation.* Are you willing to accept that you're not perfect and that you could work on some areas to make yourself a better person? Have the courage to look at yourself honestly—it can change your life.

  Ask yourself:
    - How am I relating to others?
    - How are people perceiving Christ through how I treat them?
    - Do people like being around me?

- Do others want to follow my pattern of life?
- Do I listen well?
- Do I understand others?
- Am I generally in tune with how I connect?
- Am I generally in tune with how I relate?
- Am I generally in tune with how I fit in relationally with others?

- *Examine how you react to stressful situations.* Do you become upset when there's a delay or something doesn't happen the way you want? Do you blame others or become angry at them, even when it's not their fault? The ability to stay calm and in control in difficult situations is highly valued—in the business world and outside it. Keep your emotions un- der control when things go wrong.
- *Take responsibility for your actions.* If you hurt someone's feelings, apologize directly—don't ignore what you did or avoid the person. People are usually more willing to forgive and forget if you make an honest attempt to make things right.
- *Examine how your actions will affect others.* If your decision will impact others, put yourself in their place. How will they feel if you do this? Would you want that experience? If you must take action, how can you help others deal with the effects?[101]

BIVO/COVO APTITUDE: FINANCIAL MANAGEMENT

As a bivo/covo planter it will be important to discover a marketplace job that is beneficial in at least one of three areas; money, time and relational capital. In other words, as a bivo or covocational leader it is best to choose a job outside the church that will either provide a strong financial base that gives freedom to focus on the church plant, or work a job that regularly gives extra time or have a second calling that offers great relational connections. The best-case scenario would be a marketplace vocation that provides all three. The point is that a bivo planter will need to discern how a particular job fits into one or more of each of those categories.

COVOCATIONAL CHURCH PLANTING

Now if a person is considering starting a church as a covocational planter, securing additional salary support will probably not be a concern. Instead, a covo church planter will need to be able to cast a vision for the benefits of covocational ministry and recruit other leaders who are called to the marketplace to form a fully functioning planting team.

Finally, it is important to understand that bivo or covo church planting is not about having two or more jobs; it is really about aligning one life. It's about blending a calling to support your families and yourselves with a calling to live a life engaged in God's mission.

ACTION

1. Review the six knacks. On which of the six do you need to focus attention? Who can help you on that knack?
2. Make your own rock list. Does your list differ from the one shared in this chapter? If so, in what ways?
3. Set aside a daily time for your family worship between you and your spouse. Ensure that one of you is reading and praying with your children.
4. With your coach, discuss your expectations of what boundaries you will maintain together. Share these boundaries discussions with your spouse.

REFLECTION

1. In your own words, how would you define emotional intelligence?
2. Which of the five elements of EQ mentioned in this lesson do you think you need to improve the most? Which would be the second element to work on? Who could help you grow in those areas?
3. How did you respond to the nine questions in the section of this chapter titled *Do a self-evaluation*?

COVOCATIONAL CHURCH PLANTING

4. What is your chosen vocation? Reflect on the reasons you have chosen a specific calling.
5. What of the three areas will your job maximize? What areas might you be sacrificing?

CHAPTER TWENTY-ONE

THE IMPORTANCE OF MARGIN

Researchers strongly agree on two basic principles: first, that man has limited capacity; and second, that overloading the system leads to serious breakdown of performance.

— Alvin Toffler

Boredom—the word itself hardly existed 150 years ago—is a modern invention. Remove all stimulation, and we fidget, panic and look for something, anything, to do to make use of the time.

— Carl Honore

Margin-less is the disease of the new millennium; margin is its cure.

— Richard Swenson

RETHINK

One of the greatest barriers to engaging in missionary behaviors is the absence of time—or what some refer to as *lack of margin*.

In the book *Margin: Restoring Emotional, Physical, Financial, and Time Reserves to Overloaded Lives*, author Richard Swenson provides an excellent metaphor for overburdened lives. He asks the questions: How ridiculous would it be if the pages of a book had no margin? And, what would be your opinion of a publisher who tried to cram the print top to bottom and side to side so that every blank space was filled up? The result would be aesthetically displeasing and chaotic—much like many of our lives.

Margin is the space between our load and our limits, between vitality and fatigue. It is the opposite of overload and, therefore, the remedy for that troublesome condition.[102]

> *Margin is this space that guarantees sustainability. It is in this space where healing occurs, where our batteries are recharged, where our relationships are nourished, and where wisdom is found. Without margin, both rest and contemplation are but theoretical concepts, unaffordable and unrealistic. We do not follow two inches behind the next car on the interstate—that would leave no margin for error. We do not allow only two minutes to change planes in Chicago—that would be foolish in the extreme. We do not load boats until they are nearly submerged—that would invite disaster. Why then do we insist on leaving no buffer, no space, no reserves in our day-to-day?*[103]

This metaphor is helpful when considering the ideas of missionary behaviors discussed in earlier lessons of this training, like neighboring and hospitality, because *relationships happen in the margins*. When there is no margin, it is impossible to welcome others into our lives. Hospitality toward others cannot be added to already overburdened lives.

Without margin, we are incapable of relational spontaneity in our neighborhood. Without margin, we are uninterested in opportunities to serve our neighbors. Without margin, we are unable to even think about planning time to spend with others. Margin creates buffers. It gives us room to breathe, freedom to act and time to adapt. Only then will we be able to truly nourish our relationships. Only then will we be available and interruptible for the purposes of God.[104]

But what can we do to create margin? How can we rethink our daily activities so there is time for relationships to flourish?[105]

ALIGNMENT

When people are first challenged with the exhortation to engage in missionary activities like loving their neighbor or discovering ways to be more hospitable, there is often a cloud of anxiety. How in the world is a person supposed to add more activities to an already busy week? Part of the answer is to think about *alignment* rather than *addition*. In other words, instead of stressing out about adding more relational activities to a packed schedule, we need to consider how to *align* the rhythms of our lives alongside the rhythms of others.

Perhaps the best example of alignment has to do with sharing meals. Most people eat 21 meals a week. What would it look like to align two or three of those meals in such a way that you eat with others? Maybe it is breakfast or lunch out? Or, perhaps once a week you ask someone in the neighborhood over for dinner. In many cases, you will find it especially easy to invite people for dessert after dinner. Either way, look for activities you are doing already and simply ask others to join you.

AUDIT

A second step many of us need to take is to do a margin audit of our time. Margin is not something that just happens. You must plan for it. In a culture that applauds ambition and perpetual activity, you will actually have to fight for it. It is rare to see a life prescheduled to less than 100 percent. But if we want to live relationally connected, hospitable lives that have space in which to invite others, we must learn to plan our lives at less than full capacity.

We need to take a serious look at our schedules to examine what an average week looks like. In the book *Time Traps*, author Tom Duncan argues for the need of a time budget. The idea is similar to a financial budget; the only difference is that you plan how you will spend your time rather than money. Map it out. Just as you would with your finances, identify where you spend your time. Are you overloaded? Does your schedule provoke anxiety? Is there margin where new relationships could be cultivated?

Perhaps you simply need permission to stop. Maybe you need to hear that it is okay to say no. Saying no is not just a good idea—it has now become a mathematical necessity. Without this two-letter word, regaining margin is impossible. If there are 15 good things to do today and you can do only 10 of them, you will need to say no five times.

"No," says author Anne Lamott, "is a complete sentence."[106] You simply don't have to say yes to everything.

Paradoxically, in our pursuit of margin we must learn to slow down—to be unhurried. John Ortberg says we "must ruthlessly eliminate hurry from our lives."[107] When Jesus says, "Follow me," he isn't inviting us into a race. Instead He is welcoming us into a life-giving relationship with Him that should affect all our relation- ships. As followers of Jesus, we should be in the best position—spiritually and timewise—to love our neighbors. But often we let the ways of the world dictate our time rather than the ways of Jesus.

Next time you read the story of the good Samaritan (Luke 10:30-37), consider it from the perspective of margin.

> *The priest and Levite may well have been returning from temple service and were concerned about becoming ceremonially unclean. They were about to be engaged in doing God's work and were, perhaps, in a hurry to remain faithful to it. They saw the wounded man as a distraction from what they were supposed to do for God.*[108]

Maybe their schedules were so full they simply couldn't accommodate a wounded person on the way. There just wasn't time to spare before their next religious duty. Lack of margin not only can keep us from stopping, it can keep us from even noticing what is really going on in the lives of those around us.

ACTION

1. Make a list of the areas in your life where you know you are currently lacking margin. Ask a family member or close friend to give you feedback on the list.
2. Make a second list of practical steps you can begin to take to create margin in each of the areas identified in the first list.
3. Consider both lists in the life of your church plant. Does the church also experience a lack of margin?

REFLECTION

1. How serious is lack of margin in your life? In the areas of time? Emotional health? Physical health? Relationships? Mission?
2. How might you begin to introduce the language of margin into your church plant so there is a common language on this important topic?

CHAPTER TWENTY-TWO

INDENTIFYING MISSIONAL LEADERS

Biblical leadership always means a process of being led.

— Martin Buber

If serving someone is beneath you, then leadership is above you.

— Mike Pilavachi

RETHINK

For missionary churches to emerge through the life and ministry of the people of God, the training of leaders of all types and at all levels is not an option. The New Testament pattern is clear. Every church leader should carry out tasks accompanied by another Christian who in turn is being equipped (apprenticed) to become a leader. Only as the whole people of God together develop their gifts, leadership and ministries can missional churches emerge. We will never experience a genuine church planting movement if we continue to raise up institutional leaders rather than multiplying missional leaders.

The training of an institutional leader places a premium on skills related to managing complexity, both structural and organization- al. Institutional leaders are typically trained to develop and manage elements of church programming—in other words, programs and activities *inside* the church walls. The ability to "read" and engage the culture outside the confines of the church is usually a third-level concern at best. Management skills are first, and program selection and maintenance skills are second. One of the unfortunate consequences of this type of institutional leadership is that it allows for a level of anonymity and distance from other members of the church body, which make a leader's modeling of the ways of Jesus less visible.

Missional leadership changes all these elements. The key to the formation of missional communities is their leadership. The Spirit empowers the church for mission through the gifts of people.

In the new context where relationships are valued more than institutions, the leader's character and relational ability are central. Rather than the ability to manage complexity, the ability to man- age multiple networks of relationships is crucial. Rather than anonymity, the character and calling of the church planter is known. They plant a church out of who they are and their love for a specific place or people, rather than credentials or attractive programming. The missional leader must focus on modeling, mobilizing and multiplying, all on a relational level. Organization will emerge as the church planter brings various relational networks together, but this organic development of church will naturally resist traditional institutional forms.

How then can we identify a missional leader, distinguishing that person from the leader needed for the institutional church?

NINE CHARACTERISTICS OF MISSIONAL LEADERS[109]

1. THEY GRASP THE IMPORTANCE OF FOLLOWING AND LEADING LIKE JESUS.

When we examine the teaching of Jesus, we are confronted with the emphasis He placed on obedience as the basis for discerning a true disciple (John 14:21 is just one example of this pervasive theme). A missional leader will show a strong commitment to following and obeying the *ways* of Jesus. We not only start with Jesus (Kingdom Thinking), but we must constantly recalibrate back to Jesus. Christology is not only the most important factor in shaping our mission in the world, but it should also shape the way we disciple and lead others. Jesus' words on servant leadership are foundational for how a missional leader behaves in order to enter and influence a relationship-driven context (Mark 10:41-45). The leader's character is revealed as he serves others, both believers and nonbelievers.

Another aspect of leading like Jesus is the taking of faith-based risks. Jesus was not afraid to offend the high and powerful when He was sure God was leading; He took on the elemental forces of nature and the demonic powers under the same assurance. His words in John 5:18-20 make clear that in each of the circumstances where He acted, it was in faith that His Father was there at work before Him.

2. THEY DON'T ASSUME A FRIENDLY ENVIRONMENT IN WHICH TO CARRY OUT CHURCH LIFE.

Missional leaders have come to grips with the end of Christendom. They realize the church is once again placed in missionary context. They neither assume nor expect a friendly environment in which to carry out church life. Coupled with an incarnational approach to ministry, they are not afraid to confront initial skepticism or even antagonism, but aggressively enter the context as servants. Over time, they win the respect and trust of people in the networks they enter through genuine concern, integrity and a willingness to put others' interests above their own.

A second aspect of environment is culture. The missional leader is not afraid of a multicultural ministry setting. Different worldviews provide new apologetic opportunities and the potential to win people to Christ who will, in turn, impact their country of origin. A missional leader builds faith-communities made up of converts from diverse backgrounds and lets the culture of the church reflect the indigenous flavor of all these cultural sources. If the differences are too great, the missional leader organically starts additional communities of faith to keep the gospel spreading.

3. THEY WORK OPPORTUNISTICALLY RATHER THAN ROUTINELY.

Missional leaders in the new context expect to find God at work in the most unlikely of circumstances and among the seemingly least receptive people. Because of the expectation that God is already at work, they initiate conversations, acts of service and offers of prayer and words of witness wherever they find themselves. A primary strategy is to look for new networks, incarnate in them, pray and serve until God shows them the person of peace who will help the gospel spread throughout the network. The opportunity to enter a new network of relationships may come unexpectedly, though the leader also works intentionally. Nevertheless, a missional leader is always ready to follow up a divine appointment.

4. THEIR FOCUS IS ON MOVEMENT AND KINGDOM PARTICIPATION, NOT PRESERVATION OF AN INSTITUTION.

Sustaining an institutional organization as it grows takes ever-increasing sums of money just to continue operations. Yet, institutional preservation is not a kingdom value. Throughout history, organizations have begun, served God's purpose for a time, then passed off the scene. A missional leader is cautious of entanglements with buildings and formal organizations. Though often useful tools, they must be held with an open hand, ready for the day when God decides to take that tool away and give us another. A missional leader works in contexts where the culture makes owning a building and developing a large organization problematic; it may happen, but often much more slowly than in prior days. For that reason, they learn not to depend on structures that tie up large sums of money and create boundaries on how expansive a ministry can become. Using resources without becoming tied to them is a spiritual discipline. It marks the missional leader.

5. THEY FOSTER RELATIONAL STRUCTURES RATHER THAN INSTITUTIONAL STRUCTURES.

There is no doubt that compared to institutional structures, relational structures seem chaotic. One of the reasons organization emerges is to reduce and control the chaos of relational networks. The missional leader uses organization in this way and allows it to take appropriate institutional form, but he allows the growing edge of the church to remain purely relational and learns to live with the chaos this implies. If we take a tree for an analogy, the trunk moves very little, the branches somewhat more, but the twigs and leaves are constantly in motion under the influence of the wind, and the whole tree expands as the leaves manufacture sugars to nourish the expansion of the tree.

6. THEY DISCIPLE WITH A VIEW TOWARD EQUIPPING AND ACTIVATING INTO MISSION, NOT SERVICING THE ORGANIZATION.

One typical characteristic of the institutional church is that as it ages, an ever higher percentage of its workers and leaders are deployed to service existing members and maintain the organization. The more "successful" the church is, the larger it grows, the more complex it becomes and the greater the pressure to deploy workers to maintain it. Without a clear missional vision, a church can easily end up investing almost all its workers and leaders inward, leaving none to reach out to the surrounding context.

A missional leader maintains a hard commitment to raise up leaders for kingdom movement, not maintenance. In missional churches, the effectiveness of the leaders is not measured by what they do or do not accomplish, but by how the people of God are equipped, inspired and activated to participate in God's mission in the world.

This implies a certain bias toward limiting size to control complexity. A missional leader embraces this as an opportunity to plant other missional communities by sending out leaders and workers into the harvest fields. This doesn't imply that all large churches are not missional, but it does suggest that size is not a major criterion in decision-making. If the Lord grants a large membership to a missional church, they will take that blessing and strategize on how to turn more laborers into the harvest fields.

The commitment to deploy workers into the harvest also has a broad scope. As workers mature from converts to disciples to leaders, the missional leader works to match them to their proper field. Some will maintain the local church, some will extend that church through local evangelism, some will cross cultures to evangelize and plant or some will form teams to minister in distant places. Each makes up a component of a missional vision.

7. THEY BELIEVE THE KINGDOM IS BIGGER THAN THE CHURCH.

They see the church as an outpost of the kingdom that exists to bring God's influence into the affairs of the community. Church leaders whose priority is to build the church are not functioning in proper alignment with the mission of God. Church activities that function primarily to keep church members happy violate the proper work in which spiritual leaders should be engaged. Church leaders must exhibit courage and vision in order to reorient their roles and functions around a kingdom perspective. When the people of God are equipped by kingdom-minded leaders, they learn how to partner with God (and others) in His redemptive mission in the world.

A church with a kingdom focus freely invests resources to bless other ministries, without seeking credit for their participation. They move out in mission expecting God to already be at work there and that He desires to show them how to join Him. The Holy Spirit is constantly at work in the hearts of nonbelievers drawing them toward Him. A missional church is continually seeking to discover and enter additional networks of relationships through which the gospel can spread naturally.

Leaders with a kingdom-centered perspective will speak up about a broader range of kingdom issues. They tackle big societal issues, working to address quality-of-life issues like health care, literacy, job creation, institutional and generational poverty, racism and the environment.

8. THEY DESIRE TO LEAD AS PART OF A TEAM.
A missional leader moves away from current models of a solo pastor. Instead, leadership is shared. It revolves among several leaders, and at times it even includes those who are not part of the formal leadership structure. The beauty of shared, mutual leadership is that it includes a relational group of people who learn to distribute responsibility, engaging in both leading and following, giving time for each leader to be on mission. It does not undermine authority but instead offers it accountability and more well-rounded functions.

The pattern in the New Testament church was a plurality of leaders, depending on one another, accountable to one another and submitting to one another for the sake of the mission. The church today likewise needs a plurality of gifts and input in its leadership, especially in a bivocational setting. Missional leaders will recognize the necessity to lead with others.

9. THEY HAVE THEIR OWN STORIES OF MISSIONAL ENGAGEMENT.
Genuine missional leaders will lead from the front. In other words, they will be practitioners who do not need to be convinced to engage their neighborhoods and networks with the good news of the kingdom. They will know the people in the networks by name and will have multiple stories of how God is at work in the lives of those around Him.

DEVELOPING MISSIONAL LEADERS

The previous section has described missional leaders in terms of nine characteristics that distinguish them from institutional leaders. Many of these leaders will emerge from the harvest and serve in their place without the intervention of denominational or strategic leaders. Nevertheless, North America is a place where missional leaders are needed to penetrate pockets of lostness where no church exists. They must be discovered, trained and activated effectively so that they multiply themselves through a grass-roots movement of church planting. How do we foster this process?

DISCOVERING NEW MISSIONAL LEADERS

The vast majority of the missional leaders needed for a genuine bivo/covo planting movement will not come from seminaries and Bible colleges. Leaders will be raised up to engage in God's mission as the church helps to dismantle both the clergy-laity divide and the sacred-secular divide regarding vocation. As we change the conversation about the essence of the church and the missionary nature of every believer, we will begin to see more and more people activated for church planting. The best place to discover these new leaders will be in the missional communities and churches you are starting. When speaking on the church in China, Alan Hirsch shares how their multiplying mindset can be summed up in the simple phrase: "Every believer a church planter and every church a church planting church."

APPRENTICING ACTIVATED LEADERS

When considering what it looks like to train leaders who are released into local contexts, the emphasis must be on the importance of apprenticing. From the very beginning, we need to be apprenticing people toward a life of discipleship that is rooted in the ways of Jesus, missionary formation and movement thinking. My hope is that you will use this book to train others. Walk with them through each chapter as they recognize the crucial need to start with Jesus (Kingdom Thinking), follow Him into mission (Missional Engagement) and form Jesus-centered communities (Biblical Community).

ACTION

1. Make two lists. Create one list of names of leaders who are

already engaged in your church plant. Make a second list of potential leaders.
2. Work through each of the nine characteristics mentioned in this lesson and ask yourself which of the current leaders and potential leaders exhibit these qualities.

REFLECTION

1. When reflecting on the two lists, ask yourself what you can do to cultivate the nine characteristics in the leaders identified.
2. How can you discover new missional leaders in your context? Are there potential leaders you need to be apprenticing?
3. In addition to utilizing this training, what else can you do to apprentice new leaders? How can you continue to train leaders who have been released?

SUGGESTED READING

BIVO/COVO CHURCH PLANTING
- *BiVO* by Hugh Halter
- *The Tangible Kingdom* by Hugh Halter and Matt Smay
- *The Wholehearted Church Planter* by Linda Bergquist and Allan Karr
- *Kingdom First* by Jeff Christopherson

PARADIGM SHIFTS AND MOVEMENT
- *The Church as Movement* by J.R. Woodward and Dan White Jr.
- *Creating a Missional Culture* by J.R. Woodward
- *Missional Renaissance* by Reggie McNeal
- *The King Jesus Gospel* by Scot McKnight
- *Slow Church* by Christopher Smith and John Pattison
- *The Forgotten Ways* by Alan Hirsch
- *The Shaping of Things to Come* by Michael Frost and Alan Hirsch
- *The Permanent Revolution* by Alan Hirsch and Tim Catchim
- *The Road to Missional* by Michael Frost
- *ReJesus* by Michael Frost and Alan Hirsch
- *The Missional Quest* by Brad Brisco and Lance Ford
- *Apostolic Church Planting* by J.D. Payne
- *ReThink* by Brad Brisco
- *5Q* by Alan Hirsch

MISSIONAL-INCARNATIONAL ENGAGEMENT
- *Faithful Presence by David Fitch*
- *The Abundant Community by Peter Block and John McKnight*
- *Road to Reconciliation by Brenda Salter McNeil*
- *A Meal with Jesus by Tim Chester*
- *Surprise the World by Michael Frost*
- *Making Room by Christine Pohl*
- *Disunity in Christ by Christena Cleveland*
- *Loving the City by Tim Keller*
- *Generous Justice by Tim Keller*
- *Next Door as It Is In Heaven by Lance Ford and Brad Brisco*
- *FLESH by Hugh Halter*

ABOUT THE AUTHOR

Brad is currently the director of bivocational church planting for the North American Mission Board. He holds a doctorate in the area of missional ecclesiology; his doctoral thesis was on assisting existing congregations in transitioning in a missional direction. Brad is the co-author of *Missional Essentials*, a 12-week small group study guide, *The Missional Quest: Becoming a Church of the Long Run*, *Next Door as It Is in Heaven*, and the e-book *ReThink*. He and his wife have three children and have been foster parents to more than 50 other kids. He blogs regularly at missionalchurchnetwork.com.

ACKNOWLEDGEMENTS

Thanks to my family, Mischele, Joshua, Caleb and Chloe, for continual patience with my travels, speaking, and training to develop the content that made up this book.

Thanks to my ministry partners and team members at the North American Mission Board and the Send Network. A special thanks to Jeff Christopherson for having the vision to create a role that focused on resourcing bivo/covo church planting.

Thanks to the Forge America team, including Alan and Deb Hirsch, Hugh Halter, Lance Ford, and Ryan and Laura Hairston. I thank each of you for the contribution you have made in the way I view Jesus, mission and the church.

Finally, thanks to all the bivo/covo church planters who are modeling not just the future of church planting in North American, but the present. In my book, you are the heroes of the church planting world.

ENDNOTES

[1] - Jürgen Moltmann, *Jesus Christ For Today's World* (Minneapolis, MN: Fortress Press,1994), 47.
[2] - George Hunsberger, *The Church Between Gospel and Culture* (Grand Rapids, MI: Eerdmans, 1996), 337.
[3] - Christopher J.H. Wright, *The Mission of God* (Downers Grove, IL: InterVarsity Press, 2006), 62.
[4] - Alan Hirsch, *The Forgotten Ways: Reactivating Apostolic Movements*, Kindle Edition (Baker Publishing Group), Kindle location 2167–2171.
[5] - Lois Barrett, *Missional Church: A Vision for the Sending of the Church in North America*, The Gospel and Our Culture Series (GOCS), Kindle Edition (Eerdmans Publishing Company, 1998), 179.
[6] - Rodney Clapp, *Families at the Crossroads Beyond Traditional and Modern* (Downers Grove, IL: InterVarsity Press, 1993), 139.
[7] - Michael Frost and Alan Hirsch, *ReJesus: A Wild Messiah for a Missional Church*, Kindle Edition (Baker Publishing Group, 2008), Kindle location 2640–2642.
[8] - Scot McKnight, *The King Jesus Gospel: The Original Good News Revisited*, Kindle Edition (Zondervan), 14.
[9] - Jeff Christopherson and Mac Lake, *Kingdom First*, Kindle Edition (B&H Publishing Group), Kindle location 2791–2798.
[10] - Lance Ford, *Revangelical: Becoming the Good News People We're Meant to Be*, Kindle Edition (Tyndale Momentum), 78.
[11] Christopherson and Lake, *Kingdom First*.
[12] - Lois Barrett, *Missional Church: A Vision for the Sending of the Church in North America*, The Gospel and Our Culture Series (GOCS), Kindle Edition (Eerdmans Publishing Company), 96–97.
[13] - N.T. Wright, *Surprised by Hope*, Kindle Edition (HarperCollins), 202.

[14] - Reggie McNeal, *Kingdom Come: Why We Must Give Up Our Obsession with Fixing the Church—and What We Should Do Instead*, Kindle Edition (Tyndale Momentum), 64.
[15] - Charles E. Van Engen, *God's Missionary People: Rethinking the Purpose of the Local Church*, (Grand Rapids, MI: Baker Publishing Group, 1991).
[16] - Reggie McNeal, *Kingdom Come*, 69–70.
[17] - Lesslie Newbigin, *The Open Secret*, (Grand Rapids, MI: Eerdmans Publishing Company, 1995), 110.
[18] - J.R. Woodward, *Creating a Missional Culture: Equipping the Church for the Sake of the World* (InterVarsity Press), 28.
[19] - Michael Frost, *The Road to Missional: Journey to the Center of the Church* (Baker Publishing Group), 29–30.
[20] - Christopherson and Lake, *Kingdom First*, Kindle location 344–349.
[21] - Paul Jenson, *Subversive Spirituality: Transforming Mission Through the Collapse of Space and Time* (Eugene, OR: Pickwick, 2009), 58.
[22] - Barry D. Jones, *Dwell: Life with God for the World*, Kindle Edition (InterVarsity Pess, 2014), 12.
[23] - Brad Brisco and Lance Ford, *The Missional Quest: Becoming a Church of the Long Run*, Kindle Edition (InterVarsity Press, 2013), 61.
[24] - Ibid, 63.
[25] - Ibid, 64.
[26] - Alan Hirsch and Debra Hirsch, *Untamed*, Kindle location 624–626.
[27] - Ibid.
[28] - Ed Stetzer, "Contextualization and the Mission of God," http://www.christianitytoday.com/edstetzer/2012/july/contextualization-and-mission-of-god-closer-look.html
[29] - Christopherson and Lake, *Kingdom First*, Kindle location 1625–1633.
[30] - Barry Whitworth leads the multiplying churches team at the Baptist Resource Network of Pennsylvania/South Jersey. Barry has extensively researched North American church multiplication and is

developing a growing network of church multiplication centers. See Multiplying Church Network: http://pennjerseycp.com.

[31] - Portions of the exegeting community exercise were adapted from: Christopherson and Lake, *Kingdom First*, Kindle Locations 1779–1788.

[32] - Michael Frost and Alan Hirsch, *The Shaping of Things to Come: Innovation and Mission for the 21st-Century Church*, Kindle Edition (Baker Publishing Group, 2013), 88.

[33] - J.R. Woodyard and Dan White Jr., *The Church as Movement: Starting and Sustaining Missional-Incarnational Communities*, Kindle Edition (InterVarsity Press, 2016), 201.

[34] - Barry D. Jones, *Dwell: Life with God for the World*, Kindle Edition (InterVarsity Press, 2014), 67–78.

[35] - Ibid, 78.

[36] - N.T. Wright, *Simply Christian: Why Christianity Makes Sense* (San Francisco, CA: HarperOne, 2006), 124.

[37] - Alan Hirsch and Debra Hirsch, *Untamed: Reactivating a Missional Form of Discipleship*, Kindle Edition (Baker Publishing Group, 2010), Kindle location 1341–1351.

[38] - Ibid.

[39] - Michael Frost, *Surprise the World: The Five Habits of Highly Missional People*, Kindle Edition (NavPress, 2015), 62–63.

[40] - J.R. Baxter Jr., Stamps-Baxter Music and Printing Co. (1946)

[41] - Joe Purdue, "Sci-Fi Theology: Just Passin' Through," *Red Letter Christians*, October 28, 2011, http://www.redletterchristians.org/sci-fi-theology.

[42] - Len Hjalmarson, "No Home Like Place: Seeking a Theology of Place," *NextReformation: Leadership, Formation, Culture*, May 2012, nextreformation.com/wp-content/uploads/2012/05/No-Home-Like-Place-Short.pdf.

[43] - Wendell Berry, "How to Be a Poet," in *Given* (Berkely, CA: Counterpoint, 2006), 18.

[44] - Philip Langdon, A Better Place to Live: Reshaping the American Suburb (Amherst, MA: University of Massachusetts Press, 1994), 19.

[45] - Brisco and Ford, *The Missional Quest*, 89.

[46] - Jay Pathak and Dave Runyon, *The Art of Neighboring: Building Genuine Relationships Right Outside Your Door* (Grand Rapids, MI: Baker, 2012), 38.

[47] - Brisco and Ford, *The Missional Quest*, 4.

[48] - Brad Brisco and Lance Ford, *Next Door as It Is in Heaven* (Colorado Springs, CO: NavPress, 2016).

[49] - A.W. Tozer, *The Pursuit of God* (Camp Hill, PA: Christian Publications, 1982), 66–67.

[50] - Gene Edward Veith Jr., *God at Work* (Wheaton, IL: Crossway, 2002), 19.

[51] - Christopher Wright, *The Mission of God's People* (Grand Rapids, MI: Zondervan, 2010), 223.

[52] - Tom Nelson, *Work Matters: Connecting Sunday Worship to Monday Work*, 26.

[53] - Veith Jr., 24.

[54] - Quote taken from: http://denverinstitute.org/wp-content/uploads/2017/03/In-the-Masters-Workshop.pdf

[55] - Nelson, 91.

[56] - Adapted from prayers in *Work Matters* by Tom Nelson.

[57] - Ray Oldenburg, *The Great Good Place* (New York, NY: Paragon House, 1989), 22–42.

[58] - This lesson is adapted from a portion of chapter eight of *Next Door as It Is in Heaven* by Brad Brisco and Lance Ford (Colorado Springs, CO: NavPress, 2016).

[59] - Brisco and Ford, *Next Door as It Is in Heaven*.

[60] - James Davison Hunter, *To Change the World: The Irony, Tragedy, and Possibility of Christianity in the Late Modern World* (New York, NY: Oxford University Press, 2010), 245.

[61] - Brisco and Ford, *Next Door as It Is in Heaven*.

[62] - Elder M. Lindahl, "Face to Face," Summer 2002, accessed December 31, 2015, pietisten.org/summer02/facetoface.html

[63] - Daniel Homan and Lonni Collins Pratt, *Radical Hospitality*, (Brewster, MA: Paraclete Press, 2001), xxii.

[64] - Alan and Debra Hirsch, *Untamed*, Kindle location 166.

[65] - Brad Brisco and Lance Ford, *Missional Essentials*, (Kansas City, MO: House Studio, 2012).

[66] - Alan and Debra Hirsch, *Untamed*, Kindle location 2129–2136.
[67] - Ibid, Kindle location 2126.
[68] - Michael Frost and Alan Hirsch, *The Shaping of Things to Come: Innovation and Mission for the 21st-Century Church*, Kindle Edition (Baker Publishing Group, 2013), 68–69.
[69] - Ibid.
[70] - Michael Frost, *The Road to Missional: Journey to the Center of the Church*, Kindle Edition (Baker Publishing Group, 2011), 44–45.
[71] - Ibid.
[72] - Michael Frost, *Surprise the World: The Five Habits of Highly Missional People*, Kindle Edition (NavPress, 2015), 4.
[73] - Ibid.
[74] - Ibid.
[75] - Lesslie Newbigin, *The Gospel in a Pluralist Society*, Kindle Edition (Eerdmans Publishing Company, 1989), 227.
[76] - Hugh Halter, *Flesh: Bringing the Incarnation Down to Earth*, Kindle Edition (David C. Cook, 2014), 165.
[77] - Christopherson and Lake, *Kingdom First*, Kindle location 2971–2798.
[78] - Lois Barrett, *Missional Church: A Vision for the Sending of the Church in North America*, The Gospel and Our Culture Series (GOCS) (Eerdmans Publishing Company), 149.
[79] - Adapted from Hugh Halter and Matt Smay, *AND: The Gathered and Scattered Church*, Kindle Edition (Zondervan), 54.
[80] - Tim Chester and Steve Timmis, *Total Church: A Radical Reshaping Around Gospel and Community*, (Re: Lit Books), Kindle Edition (Crossway), 59.
[81] - What is a Missional Community? (October 3, 2016), https://saturatetheworld.com/category/missional-community.
[82] - Woodward and White Jr., *The Church as Movement*, 145–146.
[83] - Eugene Peterson, *The Jesus Way: A Conversation on the Ways Jesus is the Way* (Grand Rapids, MI: Eerdmans Publishing Company, 2007), 32.
[84] - Howard Snyder, *The Community of the King* (Downers Grove, IL: InterVarsity Press, 1977), 94–95.
[85] - Alan and Debra Hirsch, *Untamed*, 141–142.

[86] - There are some who would argue that gifts of shepherd and teacher are one because there is only one article (*the*) used before the two functions. I would argue we find in many cases these are indeed two different functions in the body. In other words, there are many who are gifted at shepherding but not teaching and others who are great teachers but not gifted at shepherding. However, even if this passage is speaking to a fourfold ministry, that would be much more desirable than the twofold ministry in which the church normally operates.

[87] - Woodward and White Jr., *The Church as Movement*, 42–43.

[88] - Much of this section is adapted from *The Permanent Revolution: Apostolic Imagination and Practice for the 21st Century Church* (Jossey-Bass, 2012) and *The Permanent Revolution Playbook: APEST for the People of God: A Six-Week Exploration* (Missio Publishing, 2014) by Alan Hirsch and Tim Catchim.

[89] - Alan Hirsch, *The Permanent Revolution*, Kindle location 1110–1111.

[90] - Ibid.

[91] - Ed Stetzer, "Planting 1,000 Churches in Your Lifetime" (May 30, 2017), http://www.christianitytoday.com/edstetzer/2017/may/1000-churches-in-your-lifetime.html

[92] - Timothy Keller, *Center Church: Serving a Movement: Doing Balanced, Gospel-Centered Ministry in Your City* (Zondervan, 2012), 459.

[93] - Woodward and White Jr., *The Church as Movement*, 23.

[94] - Keller, *Center Church*, 462.

[95] - Alan Hirsch and Dave Ferguson, *On the Verge: A Journey into the Apostolic Future of the Church* (Grand Rapids, MI: Zondervan, 2011), 32.

[96] - Gil Rendle, *Doing the Math of Mission: Fruits, Faithfulness and Metrics* (Lanham, MD: Rowman & Littlefield Publishers, 2004).

[97] - Ibid.

[98] - Hugh Halter, *BIVO: A Modern-Day Guide for Bi-Vocational Saints*, Kindle Edition (Missio Publishing), Kindle Location 1036-1041.

[99] - Ibid.

[100] - https://www.mindtools.com/pages/article/newLDR_45.htm
[101] - https://www.mindtools.com/pages/article/newCDV_59.htm
[102] - Richard Swenson, *The Overload Syndrome: Learning to Live Within Your Limits*, Kindle Edition (NavPress, 1999), Kindle Location 88–89.
[103] - Richard Swenson, *A Minute of Margin: Restoring Balance to Busy Lives—180 Daily Reflections*, Kindle Edition (NavPress, 2003), Kindle Location 207–215.
[104] - Swenson, *The Overload Syndrome*, Kindle Location 124-128.
[105] - This section is adapted from a portion of chapter six from *Next Door as It Is in Heaven by Brad Brisco and Lance Ford* (Colorado Springs, CO: NavPress, 2016).
[106] - Anne Lamott, cited in Richard A. Kauffman, "Wisdom for Ministry," *Christianity Today*, November 2003, 75.
[107] - John Ortberg, *The Life You've Always Wanted* (Grand Rapids, MI: Zondervan, 1997), 81.
[108] - Alan Fadling, *An Unhurried Life: Following Jesus' Rhythms of Work and Rest* (Downers Grove, IL: InterVarsity Press, 2013), 78.
[109] - The nine characteristics in this chapter were adapted from, Daniel J. Morgan, "Developing Missional Leadership." Developing a Regional Church Planting Strategy Conference, Louisville, KY. January 11, 2007. Accessed March 5, 2008. Microsoft Word file.